KU-500-172

THE
LOVER'S
COOKBOOK

Milton Crawford

SQUARE PEG

1 3 5 7 9 10 8 6 4 2

Square Peg, an imprint of Vintage,
20 Vauxhall Bridge Road,
London SW1V 2SA

Square Peg is part of the Penguin Random House group of companies whose
addresses can be found at global.penguinrandomhouse.com.

Copyright © Milton Crawford 2016
Design copyright © Make Ready Studio and Matt Baxter 2016
Illustration copyright © Matt Baxter (figures), Katie Morgan (food), 2016

The author has asserted his right to be identified as the author of this
Work in accordance with the Copyright, Designs and Patents Act 1988

First published by Square Peg in 2016

www.vintage-books.co.uk

A CIP catalogue record for this book is available from the British Library

ISBN 9781910931226

Printed and bound by in Italy by L.E.G.O.S.p.A

Penguin Random House is committed to a sustainable future for our business,
our readers and our planet. This book is made from Forest Stewardship
Council® certified paper.

MIX
Paper from
responsible sources
FSC® C018179
FSC
www.fsc.org

For Lovers Everywhere

I worry about why all my books have to have disclaimers. I said no, but the lawyers insisted.

So, here we go:

This book is intended for adults, has adult themes and contains some explicit references to sex. Although the recipes contained within these pages may suggest that they will lead to some form of romantic conquest, I cannot guarantee that this will happen. Similarly, none of these recipes claim to cure any medical conditions and, if you believe that you are suffering from a medical condition, then I recommend that you see a medical professional. These recipes are in no way a substitute for any treatment you may need to receive.

I hope you succeed in your amorous attempts, but I accept no responsibility should you fail. Please do not try to contact me for romantic advice; my past is littered with plenty of romantic failures so I do not profess to be an authority on the subject.

Good luck. Love is a wonderful thing. I hope that this culinary adventure helps you on your quest for romance.

Chew.
Slurp.
Lick.
Nibble.

Do aphrodisiacs really work? And, even if they do, isn't the concept of eating foods specifically to boost libido and mutual pleasure a bit old-school? After all, these days both men and women can pop a pill to produce the desired effect. So this book is not so much concerned with the direct impacts of aphrodisiacs, which are not always quantifiable, as with the idea of making food in the name of love. And of course there is the hope that, at some point, the effort of making food may gain some form of reward. If you know what I mean.

But why, you may ask, would you not simply go to a romantic restaurant with your love interest and choose a suitably sublime menu? That is surely just as romantic as cooking for them? I beg to differ. For one thing, it is more of a gift to create something from scratch; to conceive, buy the ingredients for, create and serve a meal for someone you love (or at least have designs on) is a telling gesture. It creates the impression that you're considerate; that you care; that you're prepared to make an effort. I think you get my drift. It also shows your potential partner that you are resourceful and skilful. More and more people seem to be spending more and more time watching people cooking on screen and less and less time actually doing it in the kitchen. You can demonstrate that you have this valuable skill, which, when done well, shows off many of the same skills you also need in the bedroom: finesse, a sure touch, excellent judgement and a willingness to experiment.

And, talking of 'doing it in the kitchen', creating a meal at home does offer far greater – and more immediate – opportunities for post-prandial love-making than at least most forms of restaurant that I have ever been to. Put simply: you may start sitting at the dining table; you may end up lying on top of it.

Food and sex are intimately connected in all kinds of ways: the similar noises that we make while we're engaged in these two acts, the words we use to describe them, even the feelings that both can engender.

Sex, like eating, can be both mundane and remarkable. Both acts are fundamental to human existence and there's nothing new about either: the associations between food, sex and sin have existed at least since Adam and Eve. Don't be prudish about this; as I hope you already realise, I'm not going to be, despite my highly repressed British sexuality.

We use our hands and our mouths for both food and sex. We make similar noises, not just the chewing, sucking and slurping, but also the expressions of delight, groans of appreciation or – perhaps most tellingly – the concentrated silence of genuine enjoyment.

Then there is our language. 'Tasty' is often used to describe an attractive potential partner. Depending on your age, social class, gender and where you grew up, you might also use 'yummy', 'scrummy', 'luscious', 'delicious', 'dishy' or 'hunky' (like a hunk of meat). And it's not unknown for the expression 'I want to eat you up' to pass between two lovers (in a generally metaphorical sense, unless, that is, you have cannibalistic tendencies and probably live somewhere in Germany). We talk about sexual appetite, cravings, being sex-starved or sated. Post-coital bliss and post prandial satisfaction share much in common. The associations run deep.

But we're not just talking about sex here – that purely biological function of procreation – we're talking about love. I've always thought that romantic love needs to involve both a sense of fun and of adventure and this book offers a unique culinary slant on it, with fun, adventurous recipes that should help romance to blossom.

In conventional terms, the classic romantic encounter is a dinner date, where food, wine and conversation create an atmosphere of intimacy. Such a meal is the focus of this book. The choices we make about what to eat during this window of opportunity may make all the difference between a firecracker of an evening and a damp squib.

Certain foods rich in the right vitamins and minerals, and that are suggestive in colour, shape and texture, may lead to a blossoming of mutual desire.

The science of aphrodisiacs is hotly disputed and many claims made about certain ingredients are certainly dodgy, perhaps, historically, due to overzealous traders keen to talk up their wares and imbue them with extra benefits that don't really exist. I am not a scientist and this is not a scientific guide. But there is no doubt that food changes our mood and, even if we don't experience the same extreme physiological effects that are produced by Viagra and the like, the subtle changes that the right foods have on us can make the world of difference. For me, the folkloric associations of certain foods with sex make ample case that they do have some effect. There is usually some truth to myths that grow up around food and, as a storyteller myself, I am more inclined to follow this kind of narrative than scientific studies, the quality of which are hard to determine. Oysters contain high levels of zinc, but is it this that makes them so sought after as aphrodisiacs, or is it more to do with their evocative appearance, texture, flavour and the tactile way in which they are consumed? These are things that are hard to determine using science alone.

So let me guide you through the delightful world of being a lover cooking for your lover. This book is a homage to the pleasures of giving; a culinary odyssey that delves deeply into the relationship between nutritional and emotional sustenance. In short, it is a foray into food and fornicating.

I have used ingredients that are legal, generally accessible and widely regarded as good to eat. There will be no rhino horn or tiger penis, no whale sperm or Spanish fly. Above all, I would like you and your dinner partner to enjoy your meal, as I believe that the warm glow of shared enjoyment is as great an aphrodisiac as anything.

All recipes are for two. Modern 'couples' consisting of three or more parties should multiply ingredients by the appropriate factor.

And a final word of advice: gluttony is the enemy of desire. In other words, don't eat too much!

Relationship questionnaire

What type of relationship are you in – or would like to be in? This is important when it comes to choosing an appropriate menu for your romantic assignation. Every couple has a dominant mood or character. So I have classified six of these to provide an idea of what type of dishes may appeal to you and your partner.

This is not an exact science – it possibly only describes the six types of relationship that I have ever been in, though I hope that it is more universal than that. But you may feel that your relationship fits into more than one of these categories – or possibly even none

There is, despite I'm sure some protestations to the contrary, no such thing as the perfect relationship. Different people want different types of relationship and have personalities that are suited to different types of relationship.

For some, a life of dedicated, monogamous commitment is the nearest thing to hell. For others, romantic love is all about loyalty and mutual respect. Not that monogamy occupies the moral high ground when it comes to mutual respect. Ooh, relationships: they're such a minefield aren't they?

In this book, different recipes are coded to show that they are particularly suitable for different types of relationship. So, answer the following questions to find out what type of relationship you're in – and help to create a bespoke menu that suits you and your partner.

1. What do you value most in a partner?

(a) Passion

(b) Loyalty

(c) Animal sex appeal

(d) Intelligence

(e) Fun

(f) Hidden depths

2. What do you look for first in a potential partner?

(a) Their aura

(b) What they say

(c) Their body

(d) The whole package, taken together

(e) Their eyes

(f) Self-knowledge

3. From the following list what kind of activity do you imagine you and your partner most commonly doing on a Saturday night?

(a) Having a blazing row then making love

(b) Having a quiet dinner then an early night

(c) Pub/club/sex

(d) Going to an art gallery then eating a healthy dinner

(e) Drinking coffee, chatting and laughing with friends

(f) Discussing whether life has any meaning in a darkened room with candles

4. What type of physical action do you most associate with your relationship?

(a) Err, the horizontal kind?

(b) Snuggling on a Sunday morning

(c) Dancing/drinking

(d) Country walks

(e) Laughing

(f) Primal screams

5. If you had a volume button with values between 1 and 10, what volume would you set your relationship at?

(a) 11

(b) 3

(c) 8

(d) 5

(e) 6

(f) 10

6. What colour do you most associate with your relationship?

(a) Bright red

(b) Burnished gold

(c) Sparkling silver

(d) Matt green

(e) White

(f) Black

7. When you look at this picture what do you see?

(a) A beating heart

(b) A cloud

(c) Someone raving

(d) A coral reef

(e) Swirls in a cappuccino cup

(f) Jesus and the devil

8. When you look at this picture what do you see?

(a) A growling leopard

(b) A tree

(c) A carnival mask

(d) A pair of Art Nouveau statues

(e) An exploding firework

(f) Despair

The Results

If you answered mainly (a) then you are either in, or most suited to, an **intense** relationship.

If you answered mainly (b) you fall into the **slow-burning** category.

If you answered mainly (c) then you are in the **quick & messy** relationship category.

Answering mainly (d) means that your relationship is **wholesome & nutritious.**

If your answers were mainly (e) it means that you are most probably in a **light & frothy** relationship.

And if your answers were mainly (f) then you fall into the **heavy & profound** group.

 Intense

This type of relationship is characterised by violent passion, intense physicality, outbursts of jealousy, occasional arguments, quarrels, breakages, spillages and enthusiastic making up afterwards.

Slow-burning

The antithesis of the intense relationship, the slow-burner is all about gentle, ardent, respectful and growing love. Consideration and loyalty are key words here.

Quick & messy

A hedonistic form of relationship that is non-committal and concerned primarily with the pleasures of sex. Swipe left and move on.

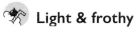 Wholesome & nutritious

This couple probably likes country walks, visits to art galleries, learning foreign languages together and eating healthily. Domestic duties are shared. Croissants are a weekend treat. Camomile tea is a nightly routine.

 Light & frothy

This relationship is founded on fun and friendship and a refutation of all things serious. Life is for living, so let's enjoy ourselves. Sunday lunch in the pub with friends. Coffee and cake after work.

Heavy & profound

Existentialism is erotic. I orgasm, therefore I am. Cue long nights discussing Kierkegaard, Dostoyevsky and Nietzsche in dimly lit rooms, writing love letters, packing suitcases and meeting in second-hand bookshops.

'One cannot think
well, love well,
sleep well, if one has
not dined well.'

Virginia Woolf

A Note
on Unsexy
Foods

Foods that actively dissuade us from sexual acts are called anaphrodisiacs. I have given details of a few of these below and you may want to think about avoiding them in a romantic meal. But this is also a subjective category: foods that one person finds delicious and sensuous another may find disgusting. Not everyone likes oysters, or steak tartare. So it is worth doing your research if you are cooking for someone, to see what foods they love and which they dislike.

Chasteberry

You're hardly likely to consume chasteberry, but it is worth a mention simply for the name. If you're in the market for chastity, this is clearly the herb for you.

Cherries

One study suggested that the mere smell of cherries reduces blood flow to the vagina by up to 18 per cent, which is hardly likely to help with female sexual pleasure. This is all the more surprising when you consider some of the associations of the fruit, especially 'popping the cherry'. Probably best to keep them off the menu if you're planning to cook for a lady.

Lettuce

This apparently neutral food in fact exerts a quite subtly powerful effect on us: it is a sedative. Identified by the Roman author Pliny as good for combatting sexual desire, lettuce is best eaten when you desire a good night's sleep rather than a night of frenetic activity.

Liquorice

This root diminishes desire in both men and women, wreaking all kinds of negative hormonal changes and reducing sex drive. Avoid.

Tofu

It's actually the soy bean that is the culprit here (although soy sauce is all right because it has been fermented), but it's perhaps hardly surprising that something with the texture of soggy cardboard is unlikely to inspire ardour.

Key

Difficulty ratings

Part-time Lover	Baby Love	Justify My Love	Love Takes Time	Whole Lotta Love

Relationship types

Intense	Slow-burning	Quick & messy	Wholesome & nutritious	Light & frothy	Heavy & profound

Arouseometer ratings

arouse-o-meter   1   2   3   4   5

1 *(lip-moistening)* to 5 *(raging horn)*

'Cooking is like love:
it should be entered
into with abandon or
not at all.'

Harriet van Horne

The recipes

THE SPICE OF LIFE

Butternut Soup with Nutmeg and Toasted Pumpkin Seed Oil 83

Crispy Sea Bass with Ginger and Spring Onions 84

Paneer Tikka Masala 86

Smoked Garlic Dauphinoise 88

Salt and Pepper Baby Squid with Garlic Mayonnaise 90

Saffron Roast Chicken with Lemon and Rosemary 92

SHAPELY VEG

Crunchy Fennel and Green Apple Salad 97

Asparagus with Crab, Poached Eggs and Lemon Vinaigrette 98

Avocado, Pancetta and Toasted Pumpkin Seed Salad 100

Pommes de Terres Sarladaises with Truffles 101

Red Mullet, Artichoke Hearts and Lemon 102

GETTING FRUITY

Watermelon Salsa with Black Pepper Goat's Cheese 107

Grilled Honey Figs, Goat's Cheese and Walnut Salad 108

Pork and Lychee Curry 110

Salt Caramel and Rum Banana Cake 112

Poached Quince with Mascarpone and Stilton Cream 114

SWEET BITS

Cranachan with Figs, Candied Walnuts, Honey and Meringue 119

Chocolate Chilli Fondant 120

Red Wine Poached Pears with Stem Ginger Crème Fraîche 122

Vanilla and Saffron Baguette and Butter Pudding with Gooseberry-Ginger Jam 124

Raspberry and Rose Pudding 126

All recipes are for two people, unless otherwise stated. All recipes call for sea salt and freshly ground black pepper, to taste, unless otherwise stated.

SOMETHING
TO SLURP ON

—

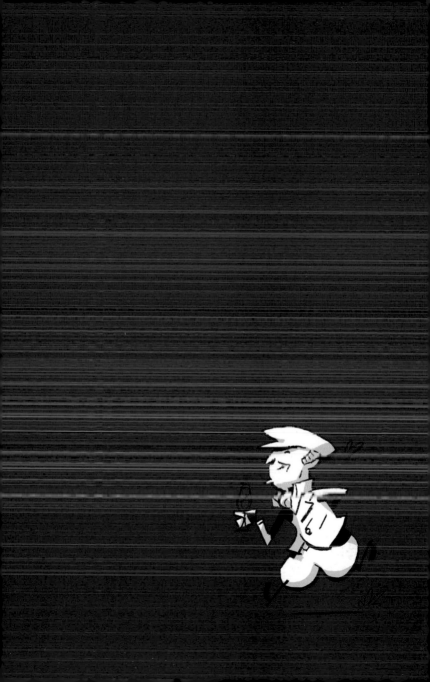

Given that I have previously written *The Hungover Cookbook* and *The Drunken Cookbook*, and that I was once Beer Writer of the Year, it probably comes as no surprise that drink should figure prominently in this book, too. Other than complete incompatibility, inhibition is probably the biggest single barrier to us getting it on with one another. Let's face it: we were born to fornicate as much as we were to do anything else, yet we have such disabling neuroses about it. Alcohol can help to pull the barriers to one side and make everything seem so much more… simple. I suppose it is alcohol's ability to do this that makes it such a problem for certain religions, which feel it leads to licentiousness and depravity.

I am not necessarily advocating debauchery, though William Blake's words about the road of excess leading to the palace of wisdom have long been a personal motto of mine. Alcohol, as we are constantly reminded, should be used responsibly: it is, after all, a powerful drug. Plying someone with booze to get them drunk and compliant is not what I am suggesting. But I do think alcohol has a significant place in creating an atmosphere in which feelings can be expressed in a more honest way, and in which many of the potentially negative aspects of sobriety – such as guardedness, prudishness and the need to feel always in control – can be fleetingly banished.

Yet both men and women – but men in particular – should be wary that too much drink may, to paraphrase Shakespeare, provoke desire, but take away performance. The porter in Macbeth tells us that,

'… *much drink may be said to be an equivocator with lechery. It makes him, and it mars him; it sets him on, and it takes him off; it persuades him, and disheartens him; makes him stand to and not stand to; in conclusion, equivocates him in a sleep, and, giving him the lie, leaves him.*'

Here are five alcoholic drinks to get the juices flowing. In a sense. Just don't drink too much of them or you, too, could end up desiring to do something but failing to live up to your own expectations, let alone those of your partner.

FROZEN WATERMELON MARGARITA

—

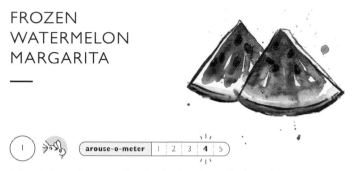

(1) 🐇 (arouse-o-meter | 1 | 2 | 3 | **4** | 5)

juice of 1 lime, plus 1 more lime for the glass rims ~ finely crushed sea salt, for the glass rims ~ 300g watermelon, deseeded and chopped into 2.5cm dice, frozen, plus 2 wedges of watermelon to serve ~ 100ml good-quality aged tequila ~ 25ml Cointreau ~ 2 handfuls of ice

Watermelon appears three times in recipes in this book and not just because it is the colour of flushed skin, roses and lipstick. It contains citrulline, which is sometimes prescribed as a supplement for erectile dysfunction. It has the effect of improving circulation by dilating veins – vasodilation – via the production of nitric oxide. In one study, citrulline 'increased hardness by 50 per cent'. Now I doubt very much that the small amount of watermelon needed to make this delicious drink contains anything amounting to a therapeutic dose, but it can certainly do no harm.

And, regardless of the impact of the watermelon, I've always found tequila (in modest quantities) to be effective in promoting concupiscence. The chilled quality of this drink adds an extra frisson of excitement... it should be served very cold. You will need martini glasses, or tall narrow tumblers.

Milton's Method 🖙 Rub lime around the rims of two martini or Tom Collins glasses, then roll the outer part of the rim in the crushed salt (you don't actually want salt in the drink).

Put all the ingredients for the margarita into a blender (not forgetting the lime juice) and blend thoroughly.

Pour into the glasses and serve immediately with a watermelon wedge on each.

BASIL MARTINI

—

(2) arouse-o-meter | 1 | **2** | 3 | 4 | 5

*large handful of ice cubes (optional) ~ 8 basil leaves, plus more to serve
~ 4 mint leaves ~ 30ml sugar syrup (see recipe introduction) ~ 120ml gin
~ 30ml dry vermouth*

Basil has an ancient reputation for perking up flagging libidos. Pairing it with the martini – one of the more potent cocktails known to man (and woman) – seems like the perfect way to begin an evening of high-octane romance. For an insight into the possible consequences of this approach, Dorothy Parker wrote that:

> 'I like to have a martini,
> Two at the very most.
> After three I'm under the table,
> after four I'm under my host.'

Knowing when to stop is a key skill when drinking martinis. So be warned.

There are more ways to make a martini than there are ways to shake a (cocktail) stick, so feel free to amend this basic recipe. I have used a little sugar syrup to bring out the flavour of the basil (made by mixing two parts of water to one of caster sugar, then dissolving the sugar in a saucepan over a medium heat). You will need cocktail-making equipment – a shaker, a strainer and a muddle stick – as well as two martini glasses.

Milton's Method ☞ Chill two martini glasses by either placing them in a freezer for 10 minutes or filling them with ice cubes. The glasses should be as cold as possible.

Muddle the basil, mint and sugar syrup thoroughly in a cocktail shaker with the muddle stick, then add the rest of the ingredients and stir for 30 seconds.

Empty the ice out of the glasses (if you used that method to chill them) and strain the martini into them. Decorate each with basil leaves and serve immediately.

ALMOND MILK
WHITE RUSSIAN
—

(I)  (arouse-o-meter | I | **2** | 3 | 4 | 5)

90ml vodka ~ 90ml Kahlua ~ 60ml almond milk ~ large handful of ice

Almonds have been a well-known aphrodisiac throughout history.
Samson wooed Delilah with the branches of almond trees. And the
ovoid shape of the almond resembles both the egg and a rather
sensitive area of male anatomy.

There is also some science that explains how almonds help to
improve libido: they are packed with various minerals, vitamins and
healthy fats. Men who eat monosaturated fats of the type found in
almonds have been found to have the highest levels of testosterone.
In addition, the nuts contain zinc and the amino acid arginine, both
of which play an important role in sexual function.

The smooth, silky texture and rounded flavour of almond milk
makes it ideal in this enormously simple and delicious cocktail,
with the added bonus that it can be rustled up in a matter of seconds.
You will need a cocktail shaker.

Milton's Method ☞ Mix all
the ingredients in a cocktail
shaker with ice. Shake
thoroughly for around 30
seconds, then serve in two
Old Fashioned glasses (short
tumblers).

BLOODY MARY

WITH CLAM JUICE

500ml Clamato (tomato and clam juice) ~ 100ml vodka ~ 1 tsp lemon juice ½ tbsp Worcestershire sauce ~ splash of Tabasco sauce, or to taste ~ 1 tbsp tomato ketchup ~ pinch of hot smoked paprika ~ celery salt, or sea salt if you don't have it ~ freshly ground black pepper ~ ice cubes

Tomatoes, chillies, paprika and clam juice all stake a claim to be aphrodisiacs and, as they all make an appearance here, this can rightfully be seen as a lover's super-drink.

Not everyone may appreciate clam juice in their drink. It's safe to say that it splits opinion. But by incorporating it, the cocktail is even richer in libidinous nutrients, as they offer various amino acids that have been shown to increase sex hormone production in rats. It seems that the same study has not yet been conducted on humans, but the reputation of bivalves such as oysters, mussels and clams seems to indicate that there might be something in it.

This is my favourite bloody Mary recipe that I have used for many years, to great success. Please feel free to tweak it to your preference.

Milton's Method ☞ Mix all the ingredients very well to make sure that everything is combined, especially the ketchup and paprika. Adjust the seasoning to taste and serve over ice in tall glasses.

35

STRAWBERRY
BELLINI

—

*handful of strawberries ~ 2 tsp caster sugar ~ 1 tsp lemon juice
~ 1 mint leaf ~ 1 bottle of champagne*

I would recommend champagne on its own as an aphrodisiac, but what kind of recipe would that be? Despite it being on the late polemicist Christopher Hitchens's list of the most overrated things in life (along with lobster, picnics and anal sex), I think there is nothing better than drinking champagne with those you love… or for whom you may yet form a passion. People may say they prefer prosecco, cava, or even English sparkling wine these days, but there is still nothing like the real thing.

Opening a bottle of champagne in such a way that the foam pours out is, when you think about it, an act with plenty of erotic symbolism. The convention is to mute the pop and it is true that this helps to avoid spillages and maintains the atmosphere in those restaurants where 'muted' is seen as a good thing. But the child in me prefers the sense of theatre of a good loud bang.

Strawberries add gentle sweetness, a romantic pink hue and a suggestive shape.

Milton's Method ☞ Begin by macerating the strawberries: put them in a small bowl with the sugar and lemon juice and leave at room temperature for around 20 minutes. The berries will release some of their juice and the sugar will be absorbed into the lemon/strawberry juice mixture.

Pour the strawberries and juice into a blender with the mint leaf. Quickly pulse-blend, then pass through a fine sieve, pushing it with the back of a spoon into the bowl to remove the seeds. Chill until you are ready to drink.

Place 1 tablespoon of the strawberry purée in each of two champagne flutes and carefully top up with champagne. Serve immediately.

NIBBLES AND
TIT-BITS

—

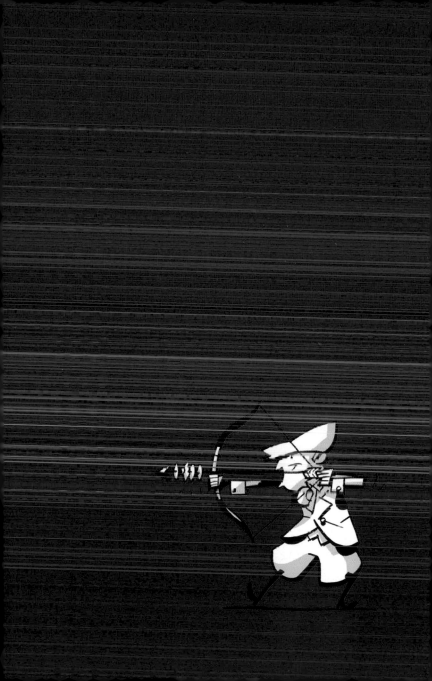

Just as sex usually begins with some form of foreplay, your erotic culinary journey should also start with small, gentle steps that serve to excite the appetite, rather than sating it. This comes in the form of small bites that aim to tease and arouse palates and minds. The very beginning is one of my favourite parts of any evening, because of the anticipation of delights that are yet to be served up. It is an opportunity for lightness and fun, before the serious business gets under way. There is something to be said, sometimes, for diving straight in, disregarding all niceties and tucking straight into the main course before even a drink has been poured, but playfulness and build-up should not be under-estimated. If all the main action is over too soon, what is there left to do?

The ability of ingredients to have an aphrodisiac effect is contentious, and there is certainly much more to creating an erotic dining experience than merely using the right foods. It is about conjuring up an atmosphere for romance and, above all, showing that you are an attentive lover. 'Genius,' according to Thomas Carlyle, 'is an infinite capacity for taking pains.' My plan is to turn you into a genius lover… when it comes to making dinner. With these first steps you will hopefully begin not only to arouse your partner with food, but also demonstrate that you know how to press more than just the most obvious buttons.

Here are five nibbles to begin your erotic culinary experience.

SPICED HONEYED ALMONDS

———

¾ tsp cayenne pepper ~ ½ tsp smoked paprika ~ 1 tbsp olive oil ~ 400g raw almonds ~ 75ml good-quality honey ~ 30g raw sugar ~ ¾ tsp sea salt

This simple and delicious pre-dinner snack combines almonds with honey and spices, all of which have some aphrodisiac qualities. Sweet, salty, spicy and crispy, this little dish pleases the senses in lots of different ways and is a great accompaniment to cocktails.

Milton's Method ☞ Preheat the oven to 180°C/gas mark 4. Place the spices, olive oil and almonds in a large bowl and mix thoroughly.

Gently heat the honey in a heavy-based non-stick pan until it is thin and runny. Add the honey to the nut mixture and mix again so all the nuts are well coated.

Line a baking tray with greaseproof paper and empty the nuts out on to the tray, spreading them out so they form a single layer. Place in the oven for 10 minutes.

Remove the almonds from the oven and allow to cool for 5 minutes, then place in a serving bowl, sprinkle with the sugar and salt, mix once more and serve.

CAVIAR BLINIS

—

3   arouse-o-meter | 2   3   4   **5**

For the blinis: *40g strong white bread flour ~ 60g wholemeal buckwheat flour ~ ½ tsp fine salt ~ 1 tsp caraway seeds ~ 100ml milk ~ 1 tsp dried 'quick' or 'fast action' yeast ~ 1 large free-range egg, lightly beaten ~ 70g sour cream ~ unsalted butter, to fry* **For the topping:** *230g sour cream ~ handful of chives ~ caviar/roe of your choice*

Caviar is a prestige food and its association with that most effective of aphrodisiacs – money – is often, on its own, enough to produce the required response. Scarcity is not its only appeal: caviar's texture and flavour are sublime, and it is also incredibly rich in nutrients. 'Wit ought to be a glorious treat like caviar,' said Noel Coward; 'never spread it about like marmalade.'

There is no greater fertility symbol than the egg and, in each mouthful of caviar, you may consume a hundred or more of them. Assuming that your budget may not quite stretch to the real thing, or at least not on a regular basis, there are alternatives at a more realistic price, which still contain a similar amount of key aphrodisiac components such as selenium, iron and magnesium as well as the amino acids arginine and histidine. So consider pink salmon roe, or black lumpfish caviar. They are less delicate and refined than the real deal, it is true, but also much cheaper.

Oligarchs and royalty may consume caviar by the mother-of-pearl spoonful, but a blini – a Russian buckwheat pancake – is a perfectly adequate receptacle for the rest of us. And wheeling out a dozen blinis topped with sour cream and fish eggs always creates a sense of occasion. Feel free to buy your blinis from the shop; however, if you want to impress your guest, try making them from scratch.

Milton's Method  For the blinis, tip both types of flour, the salt and caraway seeds into a mixing bowl. Place the milk in a small pan and heat it gently until it begins to bubble, then immediately take it off the heat and stir in the yeast with a balloon whisk, followed by the egg and sour cream, making sure all the ingredients are well incorporated. Slowly pour the milk mixture into the bowl of flour, stirring, until you have a smooth batter. Cover with cling film and leave for an hour or two. The mixture should thicken and some bubbles begin to appear.

When you are ready to cook the blinis, heat a large, heavy-based frying pan over a medium heat and melt the butter in it. Use a teaspoon to gently place small circles of batter in the pan, being careful not to crowd them. Cook for around 2 minutes until golden, then flip and cook the other sides until they, too, are golden. Allow to cool on a wire rack while you cook the rest of the batter.

Dress each blini with sour cream, chives and caviar and serve on a platter.

PUGLIA BROAD BEAN DIP

arouse-o-meter | 1 | **2** | 3 | 4 | 5

350g dried split broad (fava) beans ~ 2 large old potatoes, peeled and chopped into large cubes ~ sea salt and freshly ground black pepper ~ 2 garlic cloves, very finely chopped or crushed ~ 125ml extra virgin olive oil ~ juice of ½ lemon

Broad beans, called fava beans in many places in the world, are perhaps among the more unlikely – if not outright unsexy – of aphrodisiacs. Well known across the Mediterranean countries as a peasant food, they historically provided a cheap source of protein. However, they also contain fortifying iron and a chemical called levodopa, which helps to produce dopamine in the brain, a hormone that drives us to seek out pleasure. Whether or not the beans contain enough of this to make a substantial impact is debatable, but its reputation suggests that it does. And, as a dip, this dish can satisfy any Freudian oral-stage fixations that you may have, rehearsing the same compulsive behaviours that you may wish to repeat a little later in the evening.

In the heel of Italy's boot, in the province of Puglia, broad beans have traditionally been turned into a version of this purée, commonly served as part of a spread of antipasti, or as a dish in its own right. You could use fresh broad beans to produce a green purée, but I have stuck with the classic Puglian version.

Milton's Method 🖙 Tip the broad beans and potatoes into a large saucepan and cover with cold water. Bring to the boil, though do not stir, and simmer over a medium heat for around 10 minutes. Now drain and refill the pan with clean water and 1 teaspoon of salt. Return to the boil and simmer for a further 25–35 minutes, until the beans have broken down in texture. Drain and, using a hand-held blender, blitz them to a smooth consistency.

In a separate pan, gently sauté the garlic in 1 tablespoon of the olive oil and, when it softens, add it to the bean mix. Over a very low heat, gradually drizzle in the rest of the olive oil, while stirring the mixture fairly vigorously in order to prevent it from splitting. When all the oil has been incorporated, add the lemon juice and pepper and adjust the seasoning to taste.

Place in a bowl and allow to cool before serving with carrot batons and breadsticks.

OYSTER FRITTERS

WITH ROCKET AND
WASABI MAYONNAISE

For the mayonnaise: *1 tsp wasabi paste ~ 2 medium free-range egg yolks, at room temperature ~ pinch of sea salt ~ 250ml sunflower oil ~ 25ml extra virgin olive oil ~ 1 tbsp lemon juice ~ handful of rocket, roughly chopped* **For the fritters:** *150g plain flour ~ pinch of fine salt ~ 1 free-range egg, lightly beaten ~ 150ml beer (ale) ~ 12 very fresh oysters ~ sunflower oil, to deep-fry*

I will assume that you know about oysters being among the most potent of libido-boosters, and I examine their reputation in more detail on page 53. Perhaps less well known is that both rocket and wasabi have also been ascribed aphrodisiac properties.

Whereas lettuce has since ancient times been known to cause lethargy, rocket is its counterbalance. In a poem ascribed to Virgil, the poet declares that 'rocket excites the sexual desire of drowsy people'. This is perhaps not surprising, given rocket's pungent, peppery flavour that stimulates the taste buds and, by extension, other bits of the body.

The same basic principle applies to wasabi, a Japanese plant which tastes somewhere between horseradish and hot mustard. Unlike chilli, it targets the sinuses more than the lips and tongue. And also unlike chilli, wasabi's heat quickly diminishes and can be washed away with water. But by then it has already increased the heart rate and dilated the blood vessels enough to achieve a potentially libidinous effect.

Milton's Method 🍴 Begin by preparing
the mayonnaise. In a large mixing bowl,
whisk the wasabi and egg yolks together
with the salt until everything is well-blended
and the salt has dissolved. Add the sunflower oil in a very thin
continuous stream, whisking the whole time. Be careful at this stage:
the mixture needs to emulsify and thicken as you go. As the mixture
gets thicker, you can increase the rate at which you pour in the oil
until you have the amount of mayonnaise you need, finishing with
the extra virgin oil, for a bit of flavour. Continue whisking for a
further minute to get a stiff consistency and glossy sheen. Then add
the lemon juice, which will thin the mayonnaise slightly, and whisk
it in gradually. Finally, fold in the rocket with a spoon.

Now for the fritters. Combine 100g of the flour and the salt in a
large bowl. In another bowl, mix the egg and the beer. Gradually
add the wet ingredients to the dry, whisking until you have a
smooth batter. Cover and place in the fridge for 20 minutes.

Carefully shuck the oysters (see page 53), discarding any with open
shells. In a wok or deep-fat fryer, heat sunflower oil to about 180°C,
if you have a thermometer (if you don't, a scrap of the batter should
immediately sizzle when thrown into the oil). When you are ready
to fry, roll the oysters in the remaining 50g of flour, then dip them in
the batter and very carefully place them into the hot oil using a
slotted spoon.

Cook for 2½-3 minutes, checking carefully to see that they do not
overcook. When they are golden brown, remove them from the oil
with the slotted spoon and place on kitchen paper. Dab off the excess
oil and serve immediately with the mayonnaise.

CHAAT MASALA WATERMELON

WITH MINT

arouse-o-meter | 1 | 2 | **3** | 4 | 5

handful of mint leaves, finely chopped ~ 1 tbsp chaat masala ~ 2 tsp caster sugar ~ ½ small watermelon ~ juice of 1 lime ~ cocktail sticks, to serve

With a watermelon you will inevitably, at some stage or another, slurp. Juices will run down your chin. You will need to wipe your mouth with the back of your hand. It is, in these respects, a sensual fruit. Yet it has further surprises up its sleeve. For a food that contains such an overwhelming percentage of water, its remaining active ingredients are packed full of libido-boosting goodies. In particular, it contains citrulline, an amino acid that plays an important role in promoting sexual arousal.

To this recipe I have also added a little spice – in the form of a tangy powder called chaat masala – and mint, both of which pair nicely with watermelon and make this pre-dinner tit-bit an exotic, tantalising treat.

Milton's Method ☞ Combine the mint, chaat masala and sugar in a bowl.

Cut the watermelon into 2cm-thick wedges, then peel off the skin and cut the wedges into large tapered chunks, each about 3cm long.

Squeeze lime juice over the watermelon chunks, then cover one of the tapered sides of each piece with the chaat masala mixture. Spear with a cocktail stick, arrange on a plate and chill in the fridge before serving.

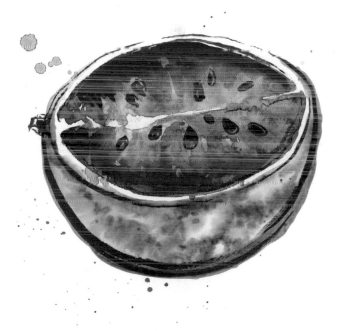

SMOOTH AND SLIPPERY

—

Casanova was a great lover of oysters. To my mind that sentence doesn't prove anything and contains two great implied and unsubstantiated clichés: first, that Casanova is the greatest lover that has ever lived; second, that oysters constitute the ultimate aphrodisiac. Casanova did, however, have a nice suggestion for how to eat the briny bivalve: 'I placed the shell on the edge of her lips and after a good deal of laughing, she sucked in the oyster, which she held between her lips. I instantly recovered it by placing my lips on hers.' And various forms of seafood do seem to have a deserved reputation for making us frisky. So perhaps the clichés are well founded after all.

Oysters are not the only type of seafood to be addressed in this chapter, but they are the most famous of all aphrodisiacs. They have in common with other shellfish a passing, though perhaps not entirely complimentary, resemblance to female genitalia and it is the textural qualities of seafood – the smooth and slippery title of this chapter – that make them an aphrodisiac as much as any nutritional qualities. According to one report, the late art critic Brian Sewell was at pains to suggest that oysters were not as feminine as many people suggest. When a colleague told him that she didn't like oysters, he replied, 'Oh. Well, I daresay you ought not to try fellatio.' However, I should probably also point out that Sewell had something of a reputation as a misogynist.

The sensuous nature of seafood and the tactile way in which we eat it, the high levels of zinc and amino acids contained within it, and its cultural legacy as pre-pharmaceutical Viagra, means these recipes are the closest you will get to sure-fire aphrodisiacs.

OYSTERS

WITH CHILLI, GINGER
AND LIME

12 very fresh oysters ~ bag of ice ~ small piece of root ginger, peeled and finely grated ~ 1 medium-hot red chilli, deseeded and very finely chopped ~ juice of ½ lime ~ 1 kaffir lime leaf, very finely chopped ~ 1 tsp brown sugar ~ 3 tbsp rice wine vinegar

Purists will no doubt insist that at most a little lemon juice, shallot vinegar and – at a stretch a couple of drops of Tabasco sauce are the most that a good oyster will ever need. As variety is the spice of life, I wanted to present you with this eastern take on serving oysters.

Much has been made of the aphrodisiac properties of the oyster. The fact that they are very high in zinc is often cited as the primary reason. But I think it is the uniquely tactile way we eat oysters that puts us in mind of affairs of the heart (and other parts of the body). With the oyster we literally kiss the sea, then swallow it.

Milton's Method ☞ Wash and carefully shuck the oysters. Discard any that are open, or partially open. Hold the oyster on a flat surface using a tea towel, curved side down, and insert a short knife with a short blade into the crack at the base of the hinge. Use a combination of twisting and levering to prise the top shell off, then slice gently along the underside of the top shell to remove the oyster. Place carefully on a platter of crushed ice.

Combine all the remaining ingredients to make a dressing and sprinkle over the oysters. Serve within 30 minutes.

SALMON TIKKA SKEWERS

WITH DILL AND
POMEGRANATE RAITA

———

(2) arouse-o-meter | 1 | 2 | 3 | **4** | 5 |

For the salmon: *1 tbsp tikka spice paste ~ 4 tbsp full-fat Greek-style yogurt ~ squeeze of lime juice, plus lime wedges to serve ~ 200g salmon fillet ~ a little sunflower oil* **For the raita:** *½ pomegranate ~ 4 tbsp full-fat Greek-style yogurt ~ 1 tbsp roughly chopped dill fronds, plus more to serve ~ sea salt ~ ¼ tsp cayenne pepper*

This makes a quick and simple starter, packed with omega-3 fatty acids that are said to improve libido. Add spices and pretty jewels of pomegranate to colour the raita pink… and the result is an enticingly sexy beginning to your dinner.

Milton's Method ☞ Mix the spice paste, yogurt and lime juice in a bowl until well blended. Cut the salmon fillet into 2.5cm cubes, add to the bowl and gently stir into the mixture. Set aside.

Take the seeds out of the half pomegranate. If it is a good, juicy fruit, you will also get at least 1 tablespoon of juice from it, too. Add almost all the seeds (reserve a few) and 1 tablespoon of juice to a bowl with the yogurt and add the dill and two pinches of salt. Sprinkle the cayenne pepper over the top.

Preheat your grill to maximum. Taking great care, thread the salmon pieces on to skewers. Lay some foil over a grill pan and brush it with oil where the skewers will sit. Place the skewers on the foil, brush with oil and put them under the grill. Wait until they colour and char a little at the edges, then extremely carefully (the salmon gets flakier as it cooks) rotate the skewers, brushing with oil once more, so the fish gets cooked all the way through; you will probably only need to do this once.

Remove the skewers and slide the salmon pieces on to warmed plates. Spoon a good portion of raita next to them and dress it with the reserved pomegranate seeds and a little dill. Squeeze a little lime juice over the salmon, add a pinch of salt and serve immediately with lime wedges.

MILTON'S
MOULES

(1)   `arouse-o-meter` | 1 | 2 | 3 | **4** | 5 |

1.5kg very fresh mussels ~ large knob of unsalted butter ~ 6 rashers of smoked streaky bacon, finely chopped ~ 2 small shallots, finely sliced ~ 250ml dry cider ~ 75ml double cream ~ 1 tbsp chopped tarragon leaves ~ freshly ground black pepper ~ crusty bread, to serve

There are many tasty ways to prepare mussels, but my favourite is to use smoky bacon, cider, cream and tarragon to make a luxuriant sauce that works perfectly with seafood. I think that a dry cider is also great to drink with many types of seafood.

Make sure you thoroughly check and clean all your mussels; a success the night before won't mean much if there's failure hours after. A little care will ensure that only good things will come of your bowl of moules.

Milton's Method ☞ Check and clean your mussels. Discard any that are open and refuse to close when tapped sharply on the edge of the sink (they are probably dead) or too heavy (they are probably full of sand). Remove the beards and scrub the shells so they look beautiful enough to serve to someone you love.

Set a large saucepan or casserole dish over a medium heat. Add the butter, let it bubble a little, then add the bacon. When the bacon has coloured a little, add the shallots, cook for 2 minutes, stirring occasionally, then pour in the cider. Let it come to the boil, then throw in the mussels and put a lid over them.

The mussels only need 2 or 3 minutes, and you should shake the pan well halfway through. Keep an eye on them and, when they have opened, remove them immediately into warmed bowls with a slotted spoon. Discard any that stubbornly refuse to open. Reduce the heat under the pan to low and add the cream, tarragon and a little black pepper. Stir well, let the sauce cook for a minute or two, then pour over the mussels and serve straight away with crusty bread and a glass of cider or dry white wine.

LOBSTER

WITH BÉARNAISE SAUCE,
HOME-MADE OVEN CHIPS AND BROCCOLI

---

(4)  (arouse-o-meter | 1 | 2 | 3 | 4 | **5**)

For the lobster, chips and broccoli: *3 large Maris Piper potatoes
~ sea salt and freshly ground black pepper ~ 2 tbsp olive oil ~ 2 sprigs of rosemary
~ 2 whole live lobsters ~ 100g tenderstem broccoli* **For the béarnaise
sauce:** *150g unsalted butter ~ 2 tbsp white wine vinegar ~ 2 echalion (banana)
shallots, chopped ~ 1 tbsp chopped tarragon leaves, plus 1 tbsp whole leaves
~ 2 large free-range egg yolks ~ 2 tsp lemon juice*

Despite having recently become less expensive and more commonly
served in restaurants, lobster remains one of life's great culinary
indulgences. Full of zinc, B-vitamins and amino acids, it is also one of
Aphrodite's envoys from the sea, come (unwittingly, it is true) on to
land to promote love and raunchiness between humans. As David
Foster Wallace urged, I ask that you both respect and 'consider the
lobster' and deal with them in the most humane way possible. Rather
than giving a tutorial on how to do this within these pages,
I suggest you check out one of the numerous online video tutorials for
the best method.

The béarnaise sauce in this recipe is a little bit of a shag to make,
but I am assuming that you are going all out to impress your fellow
diner and will go the extra mile. And a half. Actually it's not that bad
and it's well worth it: the buttery tarragon flavour works brilliantly
with lobster.

As for the oven chips? Well, how many people do you know with a
deep-fat fryer in their kitchen? This method is easier, less messy and
healthier... and produces pretty fine chips.

Milton's Method ☞ Sort out the chips first. Preheat the oven to
220°C/gas mark 7 and put a baking tray inside.

Peel the potatoes and cut them, lengthways, into 1cm-thick chips.
Place in a saucepan with cold water, give the pan a good shake,
stir the potatoes with your hands, then drain the water. Refill with
cold water, add 1 tsp of salt, clap on the lid and place over a medium-
high heat. When the water comes to the boil, leave for 2 minutes,
then drain and wrap briefly in a clean tea towel to dry them out.

Put the blanched chips in a bowl with 1 tablespoon of the olive oil
and a generous pinch of salt, then take the hot baking tray out of
the oven and place on the side. Empty the chips out onto the hot
baking tray so they form a single layer. Splash the remaining
tablespoon of oil over them, throw on the rosemary and place in the
oven for 35 minutes, until crispy and golden, shaking once or twice.

To make the béarnaise sauce, start by clarifying the butter: place a heavy-based saucepan over a low heat and put the butter in it. Once all the butter has melted and created a foam, turn the heat off and leave for a couple of minutes. Skim the foam off the top with a teaspoon (discard it), then pass the remaining butter through a fine sieve into a bowl, leaving the milky solids at the base of the pan behind (discard them, too). Set aside.

Add the vinegar, shallots, chopped tarragon and a pinch of salt to a small pan. Set over a medium heat and reduce the volume of the liquid by half. Strain and set aside to cool.

Gently beat the egg yolks with 1 teaspoon of water and add to the cooled vinegar with 1 teaspoon of the lemon juice. Add this mixture to a heatproof bowl suspended over a pan of simmering water (make sure the bowl does not touch the water). Whisk the mixture vigorously for 2-3 minutes until it thickens enough to coat the back of a spoon. Remove from the heat and gradually pour in the clarified butter, still whisking all the time so that the mixture emulsifies. Keep whisking once all the butter has gone in, until glossy and well mixed. Add the whole tarragon leaves, the remaining 1 teaspoon of lemon juice and some black pepper and pour into a small jug.

Meanwhile, bring a very large pan of water to the boil, then reduce the heat to a steady simmer. Humanely dispatch the lobsters as you see fit, then separate the claws and the tail meat and poach in the water: the tail needs 4-6 minutes, the claws 6-8 minutes. Scoop out of the water with a slotted spoon and dunk immediately into cold water, to arrest the cooking. Drain well. Take the flesh from the tail and crack the claws.

Steam the broccoli for 3 minutes, drain, then place everything on warmed plates, pouring some of the béarnaise over the lobster tails and serving the remaining sauce in individual ramekins. Season the broccoli and chips with sea salt and serve immediately.

SCALLOPS

WITH BROWN BUTTER, CAPERS AND LEMON

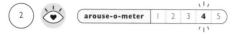

(2)   arouse-o-meter | 1 | 2 | 3 | **4** | 5 |

50g unsalted butter ~ 6 very fresh scallops ~ 1 tbsp rapeseed oil ~ 150ml dry white wine ~ 1 tbsp capers, drained ~ finely grated zest and juice of ½ unwaxed lemon ~ sea salt and freshly ground black pepper ~ French bread, to serve

In legend, Aphrodite, goddess of love, emerged from a scallop shell… and the sweet flesh of these treats from the sea is a sensual delight. The smooth and slippery texture of seafood that I allude to in the title of this chapter is uniquely suggestive. Choose the freshest, hand-dived scallops; here, their sweetness pairs nicely with sharp, salty capers, nutty butter and a little lemon juice. The secret is all in the cooking: overcooked scallops are rubbery; undercooked scallops are unappealing; a perfectly seared scallop is sublime.

Milton's Method ☞ First make the brown butter by melting it in a heavy-based saucepan over a medium-low heat; ideally, use a pan with a white or stainless-steel base, so you can see the change in colour. It should foam, then gradually turn brown. Keep a close eye on it, as you don't want it to burn (if it does, you'll have to start again). When it is nut-brown, remove it immediately from the heat and pour into a bowl so it stops cooking.

Prepare the scallops by shucking them from the shells, discarding the frilly 'skirt', black stomach and rubbery foot. I prefer to cook the orange-pink coral with the scallop itself rather than discarding it, but this is up to you. Give the scallops a good wash under cold running water, but do not soak them, then pat dry with kitchen paper or a clean tea towel.

Heat a heavy-based frying pan and add the oil. When it is hot, place the scallops gently in the pan. Cook for two minutes on one side, then turn and cook for around a minute on the other side, until each scallop has a slight spring to it when pressed, but is not too firm.

Remove the scallops from the pan, add the white wine, stir and reduce the liquid by half, then add the capers, lemon zest and juice, brown butter and a little salt and pepper. Stir well and remove from the heat immediately. Plate the scallops on warm (but not hot) plates and drizzle the sauce over the top. Serve with a little French bread and glasses of very cold dry white wine.

FLESH

—

As any writer worth their salt knows, the only two subjects really worth writing about are sex and death. They form the basis of all great comedy and all true tragedy. Flesh – or meat – symbolises both sex and death: the word carnal, which relates to sexual appetite, comes from the Latin for 'flesh'. Sexual sins are 'sins of the flesh'. Meat-eaters who have sex are carnal carnivores.

There is something primal about eating a hunk of meat – red meat in particular – and it is no surprise that the act of eating it may arouse animal passions in us, too.

Atavism is a powerful force: by subconsciously suggesting a time in prehistory before we were bound by the laws and institutions of modern civilisation, it liberates us and allows us to follow our more primal urges. Now, I'm not saying that eating a steak will make you act like an unreconstructed caveman or woman – and nor should it – but there is definitely something about tearing into meat that subtly reinforces the notion of our animal selves. Meat contains plenty of useful nutrition for lovers, but it is by emphasising the hunter rather than the gatherer in us that our lusts are truly awakened.

Here are six meaty recipes to wrap your mouth around.

VENISON AND LIVER PIES

4 · arouse-o-meter · 1 2 **3** 4 5

For the pastry: *225g plain flour ~ fine salt ~ 100g unsalted butter, finely chopped ~ 1 free-range egg yolk, lightly beaten, plus 1 beaten free-range egg for brushing* **For the filling:** *2 tbsp rapeseed oil ~ 350g venison, diced ~ 6 rashers of smoked streaky bacon ~ 1 onion, finely chopped ~ 1 carrot, finely chopped ~ 1 bay leaf ~ 1 tbsp plain flour ~ 250ml red wine ~ 350ml beef stock ~ sea salt and freshly ground black pepper ~ 1 sprig of rosemary ~ 1 tsp redcurrant jelly ~ 200g venison or calf's liver ~ a little milk*

A little pie on a plate is a lovely thing. My original plan for this recipe was for venison liver on its own, but, after some reflection, I realised that the only person I know who gets a perverse kick from eating slabs of liver is Hannibal Lecter. It is hardly the stuff – by itself, at any rate – of a romantic dinner *à deux*. However, liver is a wonderfully nutritious food with iron-rich properties offering fortification for lovers, if fortification be needed. So I decided to work venison liver into these lovely little shortcrust venison pies that make a perfect romantic treatment for a cold winter's day in front of a roaring log fire. If you cannot get hold of venison liver, use calf's liver instead.

You will need two little pie dishes, each about 12cm across. These are big enough to have a plate to themselves; serve the vegetables on a separate plate.

Milton's Method ☞ Make the pastry by sifting the flour into a large bowl with a pinch of salt. Work in the butter with your fingertips until you have a breadcrumb consistency. Add the egg yolk and 3 tablespoons of water and stir in using a knife. You should now be able to make a ball of dough. If the mixture is still too dry, add a little more water until this is possible. Wrap in cling film and chill in the fridge for at least 20 minutes.

Now for the filling. Pour half the oil in a heavy casserole dish, place over a high heat and seal the venison on all sides. Remove with a slotted spoon and wipe the pan clean.

Return the pan to the heat and add the remaining oil. Add the bacon, cooking until it is beginning to crisp up, then add the onion, carrot and bay leaf. Stir a few times and cook for around 5 minutes, then reduce the heat to medium, stir in the flour until well mixed, then pour in the red wine. Stir in and reduce a little, then add the stock, salt and pepper and rosemary. Bring to the boil, return the meat (but not the liver) to the pan and reduce the heat to a simmer. Leave to simmer for 80 minutes with the lid on, then add the redcurrant jelly, stir well and check the seasoning, adjusting it if necessary. Leave to cool and thicken a little, then remove the rosemary twig and the bay leaf.

Preheat the oven to 210°C/gas mark 6½.

Make the pastry cases by rolling out the pastry and cutting out four discs for the pie lids and bases. Place a round of the pastry in each pie dish, tucking it snugly in with your fingers. Press the pastry firmly around the rim of the dish and trim any excess with a knife, then fill with the venison using a slotted spoon. Cut the liver and add this to the mix, topping up with a little of the cooking liquid (but reserve some to make the gravy).

Brush a little beaten egg onto the pastry rim of each pie and add the pie lids, seal and crimp the edges, and brush with the rest of the egg. Cut a small hole in the centre of each lid and bake for around 25 minutes, or until golden.

Strain the remaining venison cooking liquid into a small saucepan over a medium heat for a few minutes, stirring occasionally, allow the gravy to reduce and thicken a little, then pour into a jug.

Serve the pies with the gravy, creamy mash and red cabbage.

BEEF CARPACCIO

WITH PARMESAN, ROCKET
AND TRUFFLE OIL

---

(4)  (arouse-o-meter | 1 | 2 | 3 | **4** | 5)

For the carpaccio: *1 tsp black peppercorns ~ 1 tsp fennel seeds ~ 200g aged fillet steak ~ knob of unsalted butter ~ slug of flavourless oil ~ 2 large handfuls of rocket ~ 50g Parmesan cheese* **For the balsamic dressing:** *1 tbsp aged balsamic vinegar ~ 4 tbsp extra virgin olive oil ~ sea salt* **For the truffle oil dressing:** *1 tsp lemon juice ~ 4 tsp truffle oil*

Beef is seldom a delicate commodity, but this dish combines finesse with simplicity to create a harmonious whole. Carpaccio is very finely sliced raw meat and can be made using any number of different meats or fish, but the most well-known form uses beef. The home cook has to rely on a different set of tricks and skills than the professional chef. In this case, it is essential to source the best ingredients you possibly can. There is no point in using second-rate beef. It has to be the finest, aged fillet steak that will melt in your mouth.

And having said that this is a simple dish, achieving a perfect fine carpaccio slice is slightly tricky. You will need a very sharp knife but, rather than trying to slice the beef too finely and ending up with tatters, I recommend making sure you cut it thickly enough to get a complete slice, then flatten it between sheets of cling film to achieve the fineness you require. I like to sear the outside of the fillet with a peppercorn and fennel seed crust to give it a bit of texture. This is a perfect starter.

Milton's Method  In a mortar and pestle, grind the peppercorns and fennel seeds a little until you have a coarse, nubbly texture. Using your hands, pick up the steak and rub the outer edges (but not the faces) with the fennel mix; it will stick well. Add the butter and oil to a hot non-stick pan and, still holding the fillet in your hand, sear the outer edges very briefly, turning, perhaps for a minute in total. Let the beef cool a little, then wrap it tightly in cling film to preserve its shape and chill in the fridge for around 20 minutes to make it easier to slice.

In the meantime, prepare the dressings. Pour the balsamic vinegar into a small bowl, then vigorously whisk in the olive oil a little at a time until the mixture is emulsified. Add a pinch of salt.

In a second bowl, combine the lemon juice, truffle oil and another pinch of salt until emulsified.

In a larger bowl, combine the rocket with the balsamic dressing. Toss well, then place on two serving plates. Shave the Parmesan cheese using a vegetable peeler and sprinkle it over the rocket.

Remove the beef from the fridge and cut into roughly four slices with a sharp knife. Place each between sheets of cling film and flatten using the back of the knife and pressure from your hand.

Arrange the slices with the rocket on the plates and leave to come up to room temperature before serving, sprinkling the beef with the truffle dressing.

YAKITORI-STYLE CHICKEN HEART SKEWERS

(2) ♥ 📚 (arouse-o-meter | **2** 3 4 5)

1 tsp finely chopped root ginger ~ 1 tsp finely chopped garlic ~ ½ red chilli, finely chopped ~ 1 tsp soy sauce ~ 1 tsp caster sugar ~ 3 tsp mirin (rice wine) ~ 24 chicken hearts ~ a little flavourless oil

I have been studiedly coy about my own romantic affairs in this cookbook, not just because I am in this respect an Englishman of the old school, but because there is probably nothing so off-putting to good eating than hearing about other people's sex lives. However, the reason that I have included this slightly macabre recipe is that once, on a remote island near Borneo with a very special person by my side, we ate a rather similar dish, cooked over flames under the stars, and felt very much in love. When you think of the number of chickens that had to die for this to be created it may make you feel a little less romantic, but I prefer to dwell on the fact that I have done my bit to ensure nothing has gone to waste. Getting hold of chicken hearts is easy enough if you pre-order them from your butcher.

Milton's Method ☞ Prepare the marinade by bashing the ginger, garlic and chilli to a paste in a mortar and pestle. Put this in a bowl, add the soy sauce, sugar and mirin and combine well.

Wash the hearts and thread them on to skewers. Brush with the marinade and leave for 10 minutes to allow them to come up to room temperature. It is best to cook these on a barbecue, to get a smoky flavour, but you can also use a hot griddle pan, or place under a hot preheated grill. Regardless of the method, make sure that you brush a little oil beneath where the skewers will cook so that they don't stick. Cook, turning regularly and brushing with the marinade as you go. They will be done in about 5 minutes and should be a uniform colour throughout, perhaps a little pink in the middle but certainly not bloody. Don't overcook them, or they will be tough. And no one likes hard hearts.

Serve with sticky rice and salted edamame beans.

STEAK TARTARE

WITH CONFIT EGG YOLK AND AÏOLI

---

2   arouse-o-meter   1   2   3   **4**   5

For the egg yolk confit: *100ml extra virgin olive oil ~ 2 fresh, good-quality free-range egg yolks* **For the steak tartare:** *200g aged fillet steak ~ ½ small shallot, finely chopped ~ 1 tbsp small nonpareille capers ~ 1 tbsp finely chopped cornichons ~ 1 tsp finely chopped chives ~ 1 tsp finely chopped flat leaf parsley leaves ~ 2 tsp Dijon mustard ~ 1 tsp Worcestershire sauce ~ 6 drops of Tabasco sauce ~ ¾ tsp fine salt ~ freshly ground black pepper* **For the aïoli:** *½ garlic clove, crushed or minced ~ 1 egg yolk ~ 200ml extra virgin olive oil ~ pinch of sea salt ~ 1 tsp lemon juice* **To serve:** *2 handfuls of rocket ~ extra virgin olive oil ~ squeeze of lemon juice ~ 2 slices of light rye or sourdough bread*

There is a blog that details why it is best to leave this particular dish to the professionals, complete with photos of beef tartare prepared with pre-minced beef, big chunks of onion and in various other revolting permutations. The recipe is indeed a tricky proposition, largely because it requires precise execution or else it will end up looking like a dog's dinner. And a dog's dinner is almost certainly not going to achieve amorous success. So take care in your preparation and aim for perfection.

I have enjoyed steak tartare a number of times, yet for some people, I realise, it is a somewhat intimidating dish. I don't believe it should be, as when it is done well it tastes sublime, like a delicious pâté. And, like pâté, it is best served with crisp toast. To make it a little less scary, I have decided to confit an egg yolk (a very simple thing to do) rather than serve it raw, so that, when it is broken, it spreads a comforting warmth through the fantastic flavours beneath. Buy the best beef and the finest, freshest eggs you can.

Milton's Method ☞ To make the egg yolk confit, preheat the oven to 65°C/gas mark ¼ (or as low as it will go), divide the extra virgin olive oil between two ramekins and gently place an egg yolk into each. Heat in the oven for 30 minutes.

Meanwhile, prepare the other ingredients. The steak should come straight from the fridge, so it is firm and easy to slice. Some people recommend slicing off a thin layer of the exterior of the steak in order to avoid the possibility of bacterial infection. If you do choose to do this, use a separate knife and chopping board. Then, holding it carefully, cut lengthways, then widthways, to achieve a fine mince. You should be aiming to achieve a consistent result rather than the finest mince possible. Place in a bowl with all the other ingredients for the tartare and gently combine. Place a round pastry cutter on a serving plate and push half the mix inside it. Gently press down with the back of a spoon to achieve a firm circle and, once you are confident of the mixture's firmness, remove the pastry cutter. Get another serving plate, and repeat the process above, so that you have two tartares, each on their own plate.

Now make the aioli. Combine the garlic and egg yolk in a bowl. Drizzle in the olive oil very slowly at first, whisking all the time so that the mixture emulsifies, then gradually adding the oil more quickly until the mayonnaise becomes thick and glossy. Add the salt and lemon juice, whisk again and arrange a precise dollop on each plate.

Place the rocket in a bowl, dress with a pinch of salt, a splash of olive oil and a squeeze of lemon juice. Toss and place on the plates. Toast the bread, cut diagonally and place on the plates.

Finish by removing the ramekins from the oven and gently removing the yolks with a slotted spoon. Place each yolk on top of a steak tartare and serve immediately.

HERB-CRUSTED FRENCH RACK OF VENISON

1 small French-trimmed rack of venison ~ fine salt and freshly ground black pepper ~ 2 tbsp Dijon mustard ~ 1 tsp honey ~ 3 tbsp softened unsalted butter ~ 3 garlic cloves, finely chopped ~ 4 slices of white bread, crumbed in a food processor ~ 2 tbsp finely chopped rosemary leaves ~ 6 tbsp finely chopped flat leaf parsley leaves

Anyone who has heard the lusty roar of a stag across a moor on a misty autumn morning knows that this is one of the ultimate expressions of primal sexuality there is. As a beautifully flavoured, lean red meat, venison is also an excellent ingredient for promoting primal passion between lovers.

This is a sophisticated yet simple recipe that requires a little care and, depending on where you buy your venison, a little home butchery as well. My venison comes direct from source, but you may well be able to ask your butcher to separate the rack from the chine bone so you can separate the individual cutlets easily after cooking. Otherwise you will need to do this yourself with a hacksaw, which may somewhat alarm any potential partner who is arriving for dinner…

Milton's Method ☞ Preheat the oven to 200°C/gas mark 6.

If your venison has not already been French-trimmed by a butcher, remove any excess fat or silvery bits of meat with a short, sharp knife. Trim the bones so they are clean. It is a bit fiddly, but worth persevering with to make the final visual effect all the more impressive.

Score the thin layer of outer fat with a light criss-cross pattern so the crust will stick. Season the whole rack well with salt and pepper and place in a baking tray. Mix all the remaining ingredients in a bowl to make a crust, then apply it to the meat by hand, using some pressure to ensure the mixture sticks.

Roast in the oven for 20–25 minutes for medium-rare meat, then rest in a warm place for 10 minutes. Serve on warmed plates with sautéed potatoes and green vegetables.

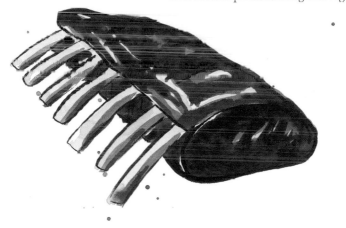

BEEF FILLET, CEPS, MARSALA SAUCE AND ROASTED SHALLOTS

—

arouse-o-meter | 1 | 2 | 3 | 4 | **5**

2 x 150g fillet steaks, at least 21–day-aged ~ fine salt and freshly ground black pepper ~ 8 echalion (banana) shallots ~ a few sprigs of thyme ~ olive or rapeseed oil ~ large knob of unsalted butter ~ 2 medium ceps, sliced lengthways ~ 100ml medium-sweet Marsala ~ 250ml beef stock

This rich, indulgent main course features some beautiful ingredients that complement one another perfectly. And the cep (also known as the porcini) is as worthy of attention here as the fillet steak. This is truly the king of mushrooms. When I am foraging in the forest and I see a cep it sends a quiver of excitement through me. The Romans attributed aphrodisiac qualities to the cep and – with its firm, bulbous stem thrusting powerfully from the earth – there is something innately sexual about it. Unlike many other fungi it is not slippery or delicate, but dry and robust. This is matched by its flavour, a fantastic accompaniment to a good, well-aged fillet steak. Depending on the season, you may not be able to find fresh ceps, but it is possible to buy them frozen from online retailers.

There are only three ways to cook this steak: rare, medium-rare or ruined. I would opt for one of the two former options. The dish goes well with Pommes de Terre Sarladaises with Truffles (see page 105). You could also have Crunchy Fennel and Green Apple Salad (see page 101) as a side dish to lighten the meal, or just some greens such as spinach or Swiss chard.

Milton's Method ☞ Preheat the oven to 160°C/gas mark 3. Rub the steaks well with salt and pepper and set aside.

Chop the ends off the shallots but leave the skins on. Place on a small baking tray with the thyme and 1 tablespoon of oil. Give the tray a shake to make sure all the shallots are coated in oil, then cook for 35 minutes.

When the shallots are almost ready, heat a frying pan over a medium-high heat and add most of the butter and a glug more oil. When the butter is bubbling, place in the fillet steaks and press down slightly so they sizzle. Fry for 2-3 minutes on each side. When you turn the steaks, add the ceps to the pan with a little more butter. Cook these evenly on both sides so they colour a little.

Once cooked, remove the steaks and ceps and leave in a warm place to rest while you make the sauce. Remove the shallots from the oven, squeeze them from their skins and reserve half of them. Use a fork and a sharp knife to finely chop the other half. Add the Marsala to the pan over a medium heat to deglaze it, then add the stock and chopped shallots. Allow to reduce by half, then strain into a jug through a fine sieve.

Put the steaks and ceps on to warm plates. Add the reserved shallots with a drizzle of oil and a pinch of salt and pour on the sauce. Serve immediately.

THE SPICE
OF LIFE

—

Spices can scintillate not just our taste buds but our minds and libidos, too. By spices, I am referring to a wide category of plant-based pungent or aromatic substances, including garlic, onions, ginger and chilli, or saffron, nutmeg, pepper and paprika, to name a paltry few. Many of these substances are categorised by strict adherents to Hinduism as having undesirable effects on the body and mind. Garlic and onions, for instance, are both said to stimulate the nervous system to such a degree that they are incompatible with vows of celibacy. Garlic, in particular, is said to exert a powerful effect and is credited with invigorating a waning sexual appetite.

My theory about spices is that they help to enliven food and, as they do so, they also enliven us. An appetite for spice is an appetite for life. Spices pep us up. They can be fiery, fragrant or intense, or all three, and offer infinite variety in the way they can be used. And, for westerners at least, there is still a sense of exciting exoticism surrounding many spices, with their power to transform a dish into something redolent of steamy, far-away climes.

Spices need to be handled with care. Too much chilli, for instance, is definitely a passion killer; you'll end up panting and sweating for all the wrong reasons. And if you are handling chilli and expecting a romantic encounter later on, you ought to take special precautions: one dinner of mine ended in painful disappointment because of my inattention in this respect. If you don't find them to be too much of a passion killer (or too sinister), perhaps invest in some latex gloves for chopping your chilli?

Spice up your sex life with these recipes.

BUTTERNUT SOUP

WITH NUTMEG AND
TOASTED PUMPKIN SEED OIL

glug of olive oil ~ 1 tbsp fennel seeds ~ 2 onions, chopped ~ 1 fennel bulb, outer leaves and core removed, chopped ~ 3 garlic cloves, finely chopped ~ 1 butternut squash, peeled and chopped into 2.5cm dice ~ 1 tsp hot smoked paprika ~ 450ml chicken or vegetable stock, plus more if needed (optional) ~ sea salt and freshly ground black pepper ~ 1 tsp freshly grated nutmeg ~ toasted pumpkin seed oil, to serve

This soup includes a number of aphrodisiacs. Nutmeg has been used as an aphrodisiac in Asia. And in Germany there was, I have read, a rather dubious folk tradition involving a woman swallowing and passing out a whole nutmeg in order to snare a lover, that I shan't share fully with you here for fear of putting you off your food.

A drizzle of shiny, green black toasted pumpkin-seed oil on top makes this bowl of soup look as good as it tastes.

Milton's Method ☞ Add the oil to a large, heavy-based saucepan. Place over a medium heat. Add the fennel seeds and cook for 1 minute. Then add the onions, fennel and garlic and stir well. Put the lid on and cook for 5 minutes, stirring occasionally, until the fennel and onions have softened a little. Add the squash and the paprika and increase the heat a little to medium-high. Stir and let the onions colour a little. Be careful not to let them burn. Add the stock, season and reduce the heat to medium. Simmer for 15–20 minutes or until the squash is tender, but not falling apart.

Ladle the mixture into a blender and whizz until well liquidised. Return to the pan, check and adjust the seasoning. If the soup is too thick, add a little more liquid (water or stock). Stir well and serve in warm bowls with crusty bread, with the nutmeg grated on top and drizzled with toasted pumpkin seed oil.

CRISPY SEA BASS

WITH GINGER AND
SPRING ONIONS

___

(2)   arouse-o-meter | 1 | **2** | 3 | 4 | 5 |

4 sea bass fillets, around 125g each ~ sea salt and freshly ground black pepper ~ glug of sunflower, vegetable or rapeseed oil ~ thumb-sized piece of root ginger, peeled and cut into fine matchsticks ~ 2 garlic cloves, finely chopped ~ 6 spring onions, finely shredded lengthways ~ 2 red chillies, deseeded and very finely chopped ~ 1 tbsp soy sauce ~ 1 tbsp bought crispy fried shallots ~ Malaysian hot chilli sauce, to serve

One of my favourite street food places in London is the Malaysian Pit Stop Café on Berwick Street in Soho. Every lunch time, long queues of office workers line up for Singapore noodles, Malaysian curries and other delicious treats. This is my favourite dish.

Warming, gently spicy ginger helps with circulation and as such is a kind of natural Viagra, though a rather understated version. Soho is increasingly criticised for losing its authenticity, but there are still plenty of shops where you can buy non-culinary Viagra and plenty of places where it is then possible to avail yourself of its benefits. I prefer the gentler pleasures of the Pit Stop Café, and this is my attempt to recreate their iconic dish.

Milton's Method ☞ Slash the skin of the sea bass fillets diagonally two or three times, so that they don't curl up in the pan. Season well with salt and pepper.

Add the oil to a non-stick frying pan over a medium-high heat. When the oil is hot add the fish fillets, skin-side down. Cook for about two minutes on the skin side, until golden and crispy, then turn and cook for another minute on the other side, until the fish is cooked all the way through. Place on warm serving plates.

Working quickly, add the ginger, garlic, spring onions and chillies to the same pan and cook for a minute or two over a high heat. Add the soy sauce, then spoon the mixture over the fish with the crispy shallots. Serve with the chilli sauce and some noodles and eat with chopsticks.

PANEER TIKKA MASALA

—

 (3) 👁 (arouse-o-meter | 1 | 2 | **3** | 4 | 5)

For the paneer tikka: *1 tbsp tikka paste ~ 4 tbsp Greek-style yogurt ~ squeeze of lemon juice ~ 300g paneer cheese, cut into 2.5cm cubes ~ 1 red onion, quartered, then split up into layers ~ 1 red pepper, cut into 2.5cm sections ~ a little vegetable or sunflower oil* **For the masala sauce:** *2 tbsp sunflower oil ~ 1 onion, sliced into fine half rings ~ generous 1cm piece of root ginger, peeled and finely grated ~ 3 garlic cloves, finely chopped ~ ½ tsp turmeric ~ 2 tsp ground coriander ~ ½ tsp cayenne pepper ~ 1 tsp paprika ~ 2 tbsp Greek-style yogurt ~ ½ x 400g can of chopped tomatoes ~ 250ml vegetable stock ~ large pinch of sea salt ~ handful of coriander leaves, chopped*

There is a lot of protein – an important substance for the human reproductive organs – in this book, and this delicious dish is both protein-packed and also vegetarian. The important aphrodisiac ingredients are the chilli, ginger and garlic, but there are also a pleasing mix of textures and flavours: the creaminess of the cheese contrasts with the tang of tomato; while the crispy surface of the paneer is a great foil for the voluptuous sauce.

The quantities here are for a main course.

Milton's Method ☞ Preheat the grill to high. Mix the tikka paste and yogurt together with the lemon juice in a large bowl. Add the paneer cheese, onion and pepper pieces and toss to coat. Once they are fully coated, thread them on to skewers, brush with a little oil and place under the hot grill. Once the cheese has turned golden on top, turn and repeat, until the skewers are fully cooked. This should take about 10 minutes. Set the skewers aside while you make the sauce.

Put a non-stick frying pan over a medium heat and add the oil. When the oil is hot, add the onion and cook for around 6 minutes until it begins to turn golden at the edges. Then add the ginger and garlic, stir for a minute until you can smell them, then mix in the turmeric, ground coriander, cayenne pepper and paprika. Add the yogurt, stirring it in well, then the tomatoes. Pour in the stock and add the salt. Bring to the boil, then reduce the heat and simmer for 10–15 minutes to thicken the sauce, stirring now and again.

Check the seasoning, then remove the paneer, onion and pepper from the skewers and put them into the sauce. Sprinkle with the chopped coriander leaves and serve straight away with naan bread and basmati rice.

SMOKED GARLIC
DAUPHINOISE

—

2      arouse-o-meter   1   **2**   3   4   5

large knob of unsalted butter ~ 400g waxy potatoes ~ 1 smoked garlic clove, finely chopped ~ 200ml double cream ~ 100ml whole milk ~ ½ tsp fine salt ~ freshly ground black pepper ~ freshly ground nutmeg

Although not technically a spice, I include garlic in this chapter because it has such a pungent, unmistakable flavour. Its aphrodisiac properties are well known and have ancient heritage: Aristotle included it on his list of aphrodisiacs. For many, though, its stimulant effect is offset by the lingering odour it leaves behind. One story suggests that the cheating wives of Greek soldiers ate garlic before their husbands came home, so they would not suspect them to be guilty of infidelity with such foul-smelling breath. I have never had any aversion either to eating or, unless in egregious excess, to smelling garlic, though I understand that some people do. A reasonable rule of thumb is that if you eat the same amount as the person you are eating with, you are unlikely to be offended.

Of all the many ways to prepare potatoes, this is probably the most decadent, though Pommes de Terres Sarladaises with Truffles (see page 105) comes a close second. It goes especially well with Beef Fillet, Ceps, Marsala Sauce and Roasted Shallots (see page 78). Using smoked garlic, easy to buy online, works brilliantly.

Milton's Method ☞ Preheat the oven to 150°C/gas mark 2.

Butter the base and sides of an ovenproof dish (mine is around 20cm in diameter) with half the butter.

Slice the potatoes evenly and thinly with a sharp knife or, preferably, a mandolin to no more than ¼cm thick. Layer in the dish so that they overlap one another, making sure that the top layer is neatly arranged.

In a saucepan, heat the remaining butter over a medium-low heat and, as soon as it has melted, add the garlic. Cook very gently for 2 minutes, stirring occasionally, then add the cream and the milk. Stir well and do not allow to come to the boil. Season with the salt and pepper and then very gently pour the mixture evenly over the potatoes. Leave standing for 10 minutes, then grate the nutmeg over the top and place in the oven for 65 minutes, or until golden brown and cooked through. Serve immediately.

SALT AND PEPPER
BABY SQUID

WITH GARLIC MAYONNAISE

(3) ● 〰 (arouse-o-meter | 1 | 2 | 3 | **4** | 5)

For the garlic mayonnaise: *1 free-range egg yolk ~ 1 garlic clove, finely minced ~ 150ml sunflower oil ~ pinch of sea salt ~ 1 tbsp lemon juice*
For the squid: *400g baby squid ~ 1 tbsp peppercorns ~ 1 tsp coarse sea salt ~ 75g self-raising flour ~ 75g cornflour ~ 1 free-range egg, lightly beaten ~ vegetable oil, to deep-fry ~ 1 medium-hot red chilli, deseeded and finely shredded ~ 4 spring onions, shredded lengthways ~ lime wedges, to serve*

Of the everyday aphrodisiacs (of which there are a remarkable number; worth investigating if you feel unexpectedly sexy and don't know why), black pepper is perhaps one of the most startling in terms of how commonly it is used. Yet is it really so surprising when you consider all that grinding and those enormous, phallic pepper mills that used to be so *de rigueur* in Italian restaurants and pizza joints? A recipe in the *Karma Sutra*, no less, suggests applying a concoction including black pepper and honey to the genitals to enable you to 'utterly devastate your lady.' Now, although I enjoy black pepper in my food, I think applying it to my genitals may be a step too far… but feel free if you would like to experiment (and I refer you to the disclaimer on page 4). In the same manner as chilli, garlic or rocket, black pepper adds a stimulating heat to dishes and is effective with a large range of ingredients from steak to pasta, from chicken to seafood.
The advantage of using baby squid is that they are tender and require less preparation than their bigger brothers.

Milton's Method ☞ Make the mayonnaise first. Beat the egg yolk with the garlic. Very gradually pour in the sunflower oil in a very fine stream, whisking all the time. Once it is emulsifying, you can add the oil more quickly, until you have a thick, shiny mayonnaise. Whisk in the salt and lemon juice to loosen it a little. Set aside.

Prepare and clean the squid (or get the fishmonger to do this for you.) Slice the bodies into rings and keep the tentacles intact.

In a mortar and pestle, combine the peppercorns and salt and crush until the mixture is nubbly but not too fine. Mix with both types of flour in a large plastic food bag. Put the egg in a shallow dish.

Dip the squid pieces first in the egg, then drop into the bag of seasoned flour until well coated.

Pour enough oil into a wok to give a depth of at least 5cm. Place over a high heat until the oil is very hot, but not smoking: you're looking for a temperature of around 175°C if you have a cooking thermometer, or when a scrap of bread will sizzle immediately when dropped in. Very carefully place the pieces of squid in the oil and cook for 60–90 seconds, in batches if necessary so that you don't crowd the pan. Lift out with a slotted spoon and place on kitchen paper to blot off excess oil.

Pat dry the chilli and spring onions with kitchen paper so that they don't spit when you put them in the fryer. Fry for a few seconds in the wok, then remove with a slotted spoon and drain on more kitchen paper. Serve the squid immediately, sprinkled with the chilli and spring onions and accompanied by the garlic mayonnaise and lime wedges.

SAFFRON ROAST CHICKEN

WITH LEMON AND ROSEMARY

—

50g unsalted butter, at room temperature ~ 2 tsp saffron threads ~ 1 good-quality smallish (1.3–1.5kg) free-range chicken ~ sea salt and freshly ground black pepper ~ 1 lemon, halved ~ glug of extra virgin olive oil ~ 3 sprigs of rosemary ~ 1 garlic clove, skin on, lightly crushed

There is nothing quite like the beautiful aroma of a chicken roasting in the oven and when using these wonderfully aromatic ingredients – saffron, lemon, rosemary and garlic – it is an even more enjoyably sensuous experience. The impact of fragrance is vital, both for our appetite for food and in how we choose partners. Both men and women spend about as much time trying to smell good as they do trying to look good. Great aromas can be seductive; they are enticing and intriguing, and smell is the sense that has the most impact on our emotional memory, connecting us with times when we have felt happy, sad, or turned on. The aromas given off by your chicken as it cooks can help you in your strategy for seduction.

Saffron is said to give women stronger orgasms. Rosemary, meanwhile, was used in ancient times as an emblem of fidelity between lovers, as it is said to enhance the memory. So as well as smelling fantastic, this recipe should also help you in your quest for romantic and physical satisfaction and help implant new – and hopefully happy – emotional memories in your brain.

However, this recipe is not a gimmick. I believe it is the best roast chicken recipe there is and saffron works especially well here.

Milton's Method ☞ Preheat the oven to 200°C/gas mark 6.

Gently mash the butter and saffron together with the back of a fork and, using your hands, spread it over the bird. Place in a medium roasting tray, season with salt and pepper and squeeze over the juice of half the lemon, pouring on the olive oil, too. Insert both lemon halves inside the cavity of the bird along with the rosemary and the garlic.

Put the chicken into the oven and cook for 15 minutes. Reduce the oven temperature to 180°C/gas mark 4 and cook for a further 40 minutes if your bird is the weight that I have specified in the ingredients list. Check the thickest part of the thigh with a skewer to check that the juices run clear with no trace of pink or, using a meat thermometer, ensure that the meat's temperature has reached 65°C. The skin should be bronzed and crispy.

Rest the chicken for about 10 minutes, so it is nice and tender. I generally do this by leaving it in the roasting tin, in the oven, with the oven door open.

The roasting tin should contain plenty of scented juices from the bird. Use them as a thin gravy. Serve the carved chicken with roast potatoes, bread sauce and carrots.

SHAPELY
VEG

—

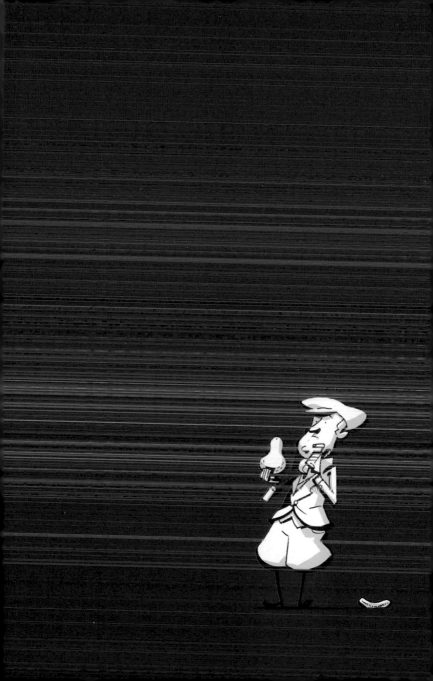

Our antipodean cousins use earthy phrases such as 'rooting' and 'forking' to describe the act of sexual congress. I'm not sure where this comes from. Perhaps from rooting around – like Shakespeare's 'delving for trout in mysterious rivers' – or perhaps the way in which a hard root spears its way through soft soil. Once we start thinking like this it's easy to find a sexual connotation in everything, as I'm sure Sigmund Freud would agree.

There is something primitive and earthy about many vegetables, and often something rather suggestive about their shapes, too. Consider the phallic thrust of asparagus spears, the protruding knobs of carrots, the labial folds of the globe artichoke or the testicular tubers of the humble spud. This type of thing appeals to the pantomime British sense of humour: the age-old pun on meat-and-two-veg; the episode of Blackadder with a turnip shaped 'exactly like a thingie'. We know that vegetables are good for us. We occasionally find them smutty and hilarious. But can we ever really think of them as being sexy?

I think we can. I am a great lover of vegetables and I think that, used in the right way, they can create dishes that are not simply nutritious but erotic and enticing, too.

A note: although this is a chapter about vegetables, not all of these recipes are suitable for vegetarians.

CRUNCHY FENNEL AND GREEN APPLE SALAD

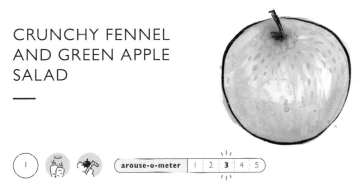

⓵ 😋 🏹 (arouse-o-meter | 1 | 2 | **3** | 4 | 5)

For the salad: *1 tbsp fennel seeds ~ 1 fennel bulb ~ 1 green apple ~ large handful of rocket* **For the dressing:** *1 tsp Dijon mustard ~ 1 tsp honey ~ 1 tbsp unfiltered cider vinegar ~ 4 tbsp extra virgin olive oil ~ pinch of sea salt*

The apple has long been used as a symbol of sex, romantic love, carnal knowledge and sin. In a biblical context, it is the forbidden fruit. Venus, the Roman goddess of love, is often pictured holding an apple. Aphrodite, her Greek counterpart, gave the fruits as gifts. A recent study discovered that women who regularly eat apples have better sex than those that don't. I'm not sure that is conclusive proof that apples are aphrodisiacs, but perhaps it more pertinently relates to the adage that 'an apple a day keeps the doctor away'… and hence to the fact that a physically healthy person is more likely to have a better sex life. Fennel may not be so conspicuous in ancient legend, but it was a surprising ingredient of Dionysian orgies.

This simple, refreshing salad can be served as a side dish with a variety of different meaty or fishy main courses.

Milton's Method ☞ Toast the fennel seeds in a dry pan over a medium heat until they darken just a touch. Remove from the pan and set aside.

Remove the hard core at the base of the fennel bulb and slice it lengthways as thinly as possible. Quarter and core the apple and slice it thinly, too. Place these and the rocket in a salad bowl and mix together.

Now, working quickly before the salad ingredients turn brown, combine all the ingredients for the dressing in a separate bowl and whisk until emulsified. Add the dressing to the salad, toss well, then sprinkle the fennel seeds on top and serve.

ASPARAGUS

WITH CRAB, POACHED EGGS AND LEMON VINAIGRETTE

(3) arouse-o-meter | 1 | 2 | 3 | **4** | 5 |

For the vinigarette: *½ tsp finely grated unwaxed lemon zest, plus 2 tbsp lemon juice ~ ½ tsp Dijon mustard ~ ½ tsp honey ~ 4–5 tbsp extra virgin olive oil ~ sea salt and freshly ground black pepper* **For the rest:** *12 in-season asparagus spears ~ a little olive oil ~ white bread, torn into rough crouton shapes ~ 4 free-range eggs ~ 2 tsp white wine vinegar ~ 6 tbsp fresh white crab meat ~ ½ tsp sea salt*

Both asparagus and eggs are aphrodisiacs, while seafood contains high levels of zinc and selenium, making this a lover's recipe *par excellence*. Just think: thrusting spears of phallic fecundity lying amongst the most potent symbol of fertility of all – the egg – with the fresh ocean flavour of crab sparked into life by a sharp lemon vinaigrette that brings everything together. This makes an excellent starter or a weekend brunch/lunch in preparation for a spot of frisky afternoon fun.

Asparagus, apart from looking the part, also contains lots of useful vitamins that are helpful for boosting libido and general vim and vigour. The one well-known side effect of asparagus that does make it a bit of a turn-off (smelly wee) means that you should open the window after you have urinated.

Milton's Method ☞ Start by making the vinaigrette. In a small bowl, whisk the lemon zest and juice, mustard and honey together with a small whisk or fork. Drizzle in the olive oil slowly so the mixture emulsifies, then season to taste. Set aside.

Using the freshest asparagus you can find, trim off any tough part of the stem at the base, wash and place in a steamer. Steam for around 3 minutes until just tender, but still with some bite. Do not overcook: limpness is not a good look.

Heat some regular olive oil in a frying pan and fry the bread until golden. Drain the croutons on a plate lined with kitchen paper.

Meanwhile, crack open the eggs and place each into a cup. Put the vinegar into a large pan of water and heat it until there are small bubbles rising to the surface. Reduce the heat to medium low and swirl the water round with a spoon. Place the eggs in this whirlpool one at a time and cook for 3–4 minutes, or until the whites are set. Gently drain the eggs and run cold water over them for a few seconds so they stop cooking. This should be the very last thing you do, as the eggs need to be still warm when they are eaten.

On a single warmed platter, or two large warmed plates, roughly scatter the asparagus, seasoning it with the ½ tsp of salt, then add the crab meat. Place the eggs on top, sprinkle over the vinaigrette and croutons and serve immediately.

AVOCADO, PANCETTA AND TOASTED PUMPKIN SEED SALAD

—

2 ·  · arouse-o-meter | 1 | **2** | 3 | 4 | 5 |

10 very thin slices of pancetta ~ 1 tbsp white wine vinegar ~ 4 tbsp toasted pumpkin seed oil ~ pinch of sea salt ~ 2 handfuls of baby spinach ~ 2 perfectly ripe Haas avocados ~ 2 tbsp pumpkin seeds

Pumpkin seeds are packed with zinc, an important mineral for amorousness, and are included here in two ways: both sprinkled on top of this simple salad and as a key ingredient of the dressing. Toasted pumpkin seed oil is absolutely delicious, but expensive and not widely available, though you can find it in health food shops. Make sure you only use perfectly ripe avocados. Packed with nutrition, these are also well known as aphrodisiacs.

Milton's Method ☞ Put the pancetta under a hot grill and cook for around 4 minutes, watching carefully to make sure it doesn't burn, turning once, and removing when crisp.

Make the dressing by combining the vinegar, pumpkin seed oil and salt in a bowl and whisking until well blended.

Put the spinach in a bowl and add half the dressing, tossing thoroughly. Place on two plates.

Prepare the avocados by cutting in half, peeling and removing the stones. Cut into 1cm-thick slices and place them gently on the spinach. Arrange the crispy pancetta on top.

Toast the pumpkin seeds in a dry frying pan for around 3 minutes until they begin to colour and pop. Sprinkle over the salad, then drizzle the remaining dressing over the top.

POMMES DE TERRES
SARLADAISES

WITH TRUFFLES

(2)   arouse-o-meter | 1 | **2** | 3 | 4 | 5 |

3 large potatoes ~ 1 tbsp goose or duck fat ~ sea salt and freshly ground black pepper ~ 1 tbsp finely chopped flat leaf parsley leaves ~ 10g black truffle, shaved, or truffle salt

A favourite way of cooking potatoes in the south west of France, the secret here is to use goose or duck fat rather than butter or oil. The dish is sometimes combined with another favourite of French cooking: truffle. A byword for indulgence, the truffle has an aroma and flavour unlike anything else, a rich, perfumed earthiness that has for centuries perked up flagging sex lives. The black Périgord truffles that are most commonly used are expensive, and you may wish instead to use a good-quality truffle salt.

This is a simple recipe — just sautéed potatoes, really – that goes brilliantly with grilled meats.

Milton's Method ☞ Peel the potatoes, then slice into thinnish round slices.

Put the goose fat in a large, heavy-based frying pan over a medium heat. When it has melted, add the potatoes and make sure all the slices get coated with fat. Cook for around 15 minutes, turning regularly, until crisp and golden.

Season with salt, pepper, parsley and shaved truffle, if using, or sprinkle evenly with a little truffle salt instead.

RED MULLET, ARTICHOKE HEARTS AND LEMON

(4) arouse-o-meter | 1 | 2 | **3** | 4 | 5

6 fresh globe artichokes, or 6 pre-cooked frozen artichoke hearts ~ finely grated zest and juice of 1 unwaxed lemon, plus ½ lemon to prepare and cook the artichoke ~ good-quality extra virgin olive oil ~ 1 garlic clove, finely chopped ~ 1 tbsp thyme leaves ~ sea salt and freshly ground black pepper ~ 4 fillets of red mullet

The globe artichoke can be eaten in the most tactile of ways with a lover: boil or steam a fresh, firm artichoke for a good while then, together, lovingly peel off the outer leaves, dip them in butter, vinaigrette or hollandaise sauce and scrape the flesh from them with your teeth. This is best done outside, on a warm summer's evening, at sunset, with a glass of chilled muscat and someone special by your side, as I have often done. In the centre of the mass of overlapping leaves is the true delight of an artichoke – the heart – and, when perfectly cooked, the heart is one of the most delicious vegetables it is possible to eat.

I have paired the hearts here with red mullet, as they complement one another well, but this artichoke recipe can also be used on its own as a side dish to grilled chicken.

A relative of the thistle, the artichoke promotes good liver health… and good livers make better lovers.

Milton's Method ☞ If preparing fresh artichokes, peel off the outer leaves, then use a knife to remove the inner leaves until you get down to the heart in the middle. Remove the hairy, fibrous choke in the centre by scooping it out with a teaspoon. Squeeze a little lemon on to each artichoke heart to prevent discoloration and place in a saucepan of cold water. Squeeze the remaining lemon juice from the half lemon into the water and place the lemon half in the pan, too. Bring to the boil, then reduce the heat and simmer over a low heat, with a lid on, for around 30 minutes, or until just tender but still with a little bite. (If using frozen artichoke hearts, they only need to be heated through briefly in boiling water.)

Drain, allow to cool a little, then slice lengthways. In a heavy-based frying pan, heat the olive oil over a medium-high heat and sauté the artichoke slices for 2 minutes, then add the garlic, thyme, lemon zest and juice and salt and pepper. Cook for a further 2 minutes, then place on warm plates.

Quickly season the fish fillets with a little salt and pepper and cook in the same pan, skin-side down at first, for 2 minutes on each side, until just cooked. Serve immediately with the artichokes, accompanied by sautéed potatoes and a rocket salad.

GETTING
FRUITY

—

From the suggestive shape of bananas to the delicate, feminine fragrance of quince, fruit can be a surprisingly effective aphrodisiac. I've always thought of fruit in general as an intensely sensual form of food. At its erotic, chin-dribbling, slurp-making, mouth-wiping best, fruit offers treats that are sweet yet wholesome and healthy yet indulgent... a little like sex should be, really.

The idea of fruit as a treat tends to be a little overlooked these days in the developed world, where fruit is seen in general as less of an indulgence and more about reaching a daily quota of dietary intake. We are primates and our cousins in the animal world go wild for the bright colours and sugar found in fruits. To a large extent, in our sugar-rich society, we have lost that same excitement. But, for me, fruit is always a pure and happy pleasure: the crunchy bite of an apple; blackberry-stained fingers; strawberries and ice cream in the summer.

The apple has long been used as a symbol of fertility, love and eroticism. It is associated with Aphrodite, the goddess of love, and in Ancient Greece it was customary for couples to eat apples on their wedding night. Read on to discover how the apple – and other fruits – can take you from the boughs of the apple tree all the way down to a comfortable spot in the long grass beneath it.

WATERMELON SALSA

WITH BLACK PEPPER
GOAT'S CHEESE

___

200g soft fresh goat's cheese ~ 1 tbsp olive oil ~ 1 tbsp freshly cracked black pepper ~ ½ small watermelon, deseeded, cut into 1cm dice ~ ½ cucumber, peeled, cut into 1cm dice ~ juice and finely grated zest of 1 lime ~ 1 small red onion, very finely sliced into crescents ~ handful of mint leaves, roughly chopped ~ 1 medium-hot red chilli, deseeded and finely chopped ~ 1 tbsp extra virgin olive oil ~ ½ tsp sea salt ~ crackers or crispbread, to serve

Miraculous attributes are ascribed to the watermelon, which is perhaps surprising given that many other aphrodisiac ingredients are pungent in nature whereas the watermelon is rather... well... watery? Being so mellow itself in flavour, however, it works well with spices, salt and herbs, some of which have their own stimulating properties. This could be a starter, an unusual cheese course or a light lunch.

Milton's Method ☞ Blend the goat's cheese, regular olive oil and black pepper with a whisk until you have a lovely, creamy texture. Place an artful dollop on each plate.

Combine all the remaining ingredients in a bowl to make the salsa and mix well. Leave for 5 minutes for the flavours to infuse, then spoon on to each plate. Serve with crackers or crispbread.

GRILLED HONEY FIGS, GOAT'S CHEESE AND WALNUT SALAD

| arouse-o-meter | 1 | 2 | **3** | 4 | 5 |

For the salad: *8 round slices from a small baguette ~ olive oil ~ 4 perfectly ripe figs ~ 1 tbsp honey ~ 2 pinches of sea salt ~ 8 x 1cm-thick round slices of goat's cheese ~ 2 large handfuls of mixed salad leaves ~ handful of walnuts*
For the dressing: *1 tsp Dijon mustard ~ 1 tsp honey ~ 1 tbsp white wine vinegar ~ 4 tbsp extra virgin olive oil*

Nudity is probably never far from our minds when the word 'fig' is mentioned, as we reach in our minds for a metaphorical fig leaf… Though please don't misunderstand me: I have never liked the idea of naked dining. There is a time and place for everything and nudity at the dinner table strikes me as the wrong time and the wrong place, at least while food is being served. It's a little like breakfast in bed: why would you want big flaky croissant crumbs – or sharp, nasty toast crumbs – pricking you on your smooth sheets?

Figs are a luscious fruit and a well-known aphrodisiac. In ripe, tender splendour they are a deep, priapic shade of purple. They go well with sharp, creamy goat's cheese and this simple dish makes an excellent starter or light lunch.

Milton's Method ☞ Brush each of the pieces of baguette on both sides with a little olive oil and place under a medium grill for around 2 minutes on each side, until golden and crisp. Set aside.

Cut the figs in half and place on the grill pan, cut sides up. Loosen the honey with 1 tsp of hot water, add a pinch of salt, then brush the figs with the honey mixture and place under a medium grill for 5 minutes. Set aside.

Place the slices of goat's cheese on the slices of crispy bread. Put under the grill (now medium-hot) for a few minutes, until the cheese colours on top.

Meanwhile, place the leaves in a salad bowl. Make the dressing by combining the mustard, honey and vinegar in a separate bowl, whisking until well mixed, then pour in the olive oil in a steady stream until emulsified. Add three-quarters of the dressing to the leaves, toss well and place on plates. When the cheese is done, place on top of the salad leaves with the figs in between. Toast the walnuts in a dry pan and sprinkle on top, drizzle the remaining dressing over and serve immediately.

PORK AND
LYCHEE CURRY

—

3   arouse-o-meter   1   2   **3**   4   5

3 garlic cloves, roughly chopped ~ thumb-sized piece of root ginger, peeled and roughly chopped ~ 2 lemon grass stalks, roughly chopped ~ handful of coriander, torn, plus more to serve ~ 2 long red chillies, roughly chopped ~ 2 tbsp tamarind purée ~ 4 kaffir lime leaves ~ flavourless oil ~ sea salt and freshly ground black pepper ~ 400g diced pork shoulder or chump end ~ 1 onion, finely chopped ~ 2 tsp curry powder ~ 2 star anise ~ 250ml chicken stock ~ 400ml can of coconut milk ~ 1 tsp Thai fish sauce ~ ½ x 400g can of lychees, drained (or 8 fresh lychees, peeled and pitted) ~ juice of ½ lime ~ pomegranate seeds, to serve

This is my version of a curry I once had in Singapore, which in a way represents the racial diversity that can be found there. Singapore is populated by populations from South East Asia, China and India and this curry combines influences from all three. The lychee is considered an aphrodisiac in China and its subtle fruitiness combines well with pork in this fragrant, slow-cooked dish.

Milton's Method ☞ Make a curry paste by blending the garlic, ginger, lemon grass, coriander, chillies, tamarind, lime leaves and 1 teaspoon of oil until everything is finely whizzed into a paste. You may need to squash the ingredients down a couple of times in order to achieve this consistency.

Lightly season the pork and place a heavy-based casserole dish over a medium-high heat with a good glug of oil. Sear the pork briefly on all sides, then remove with a slotted spoon and set aside. Immediately deglaze the pan with a splash of water. Give the pan a stir, then add the onion and a little more oil if necessary. Cook over a medium heat for 6 or 7 minutes, until the onion begins to colour slightly.

Add the blended curry paste and cook for 2 minutes, stirring occasionally and making sure that it doesn't stick to the pan. Add the curry powder and star anise, stir and add the chicken stock. Bring to the boil and allow to simmer for 5 minutes until the volume of the liquid has reduced by half. Now add the coconut milk and fish sauce and gently bring to the boil. Return the pork pieces to the pan, return to the boil once more, then reduce the heat to very low, put on a lid, and simmer for an hour and a quarter, checking occasionally to make sure it is not catching on the bottom.

When the time has elapsed, give everything a good stir and add the lychees. Remove the lid and cook for a further 20 minutes over a medium-low heat, allowing the sauce to thicken a little. Finish by adding the lime juice and adjusting the seasoning to your preference.

Serve immediately on hot plates with rice or noodles, sprinkled with coriander leaves and pomegranate seeds.

SALT CARAMEL AND RUM BANANA CAKE

4 | arouse-o-meter | 1 | 2 | **3** | 4 | 5 |

For the salt caramel: *100g unsalted butter ~ 100g soft light brown sugar ~ 100g caster sugar ~ 100g golden syrup ~ 200ml double cream ~ 1 tsp sea salt*
For the cake: *100g softened unsalted butter, plus more for the tins ~ 100g caster sugar ~ 100g demerara sugar ~ 3 large free-range eggs, separated ~ 3 mashed bananas, plus 1 banana to decorate ~ 200ml whole milk ~ 1 vanilla pod, split ~ 50ml dark rum ~ 300g self-raising flour, sifted ~ 1 tsp baking powder* **For the buttercream:** *110g unsalted butter ~ ½ tsp vanilla extract ~ 120g icing sugar*

The suggestiveness of bananas hardly requires elaboration on my part. Here they are mashed into a truly rich, indulgent, moist and sweet dessert tempered by a little saltiness that will serve around eight people and works wonderfully well with vanilla ice cream. I have borrowed Nigella Lawson's method for making the salt caramel.

Milton's Method ☞ Start by making the salt caramel. Melt the butter, both types of sugar and the golden syrup in a small heavy-based pan for 4 minutes, stirring occasionally to make sure it doesn't stick and letting it darken a little. Then add the cream and the salt, whisking as you do so, until fully incorporated. Remove from the heat and put in a bowl or jug.

To make the cake, preheat the oven to 160°C/gas mark 3 and butter two 23cm circular cake tins.

In a large bowl, using either a hand-whisk or a stand mixer, cream the butter and both types of sugar together until fluffy, then beat in the egg yolks one at a time until well incorporated.

In a separate bowl, whisk the egg whites until they are stiff.

Gradually beat the mashed bananas into the butter mixture, then add the milk, scrape in the seeds from the vanilla pod and add the rum. Fold in the flour until everything is incorporated. Add the baking powder and 150ml of the salt caramel and stir it in with a wooden spoon, then fold in the stiff egg whites.

Pour the batter evenly into the prepared cake tins. Pour another 50ml of salt caramel equally into each cake tin and use a knife to make it into a swirly pattern. Bake for around 45 minutes. Make sure the middle is cooked by using a skewer; when inserted into the cake it should emerge clean. Set aside to cool on a wire rack while you make the buttercream.

In a large bowl, using either a hand-whisk or a stand mixer, whisk the butter, 110ml of the caramel sauce and the vanilla extract until creamy. Then, still whisking, add the icing sugar bit by bit until the buttercream is nice and light.

Now you can assemble the whole thing. Add a layer of buttercream to the first tier of cake and drizzle a little of the remaining salt caramel over the top. Add the top layer, ice this with buttercream and pour more salt caramel mixture on top of that. Add slices of bananas and serve with vanilla ice cream.

POACHED QUINCE

WITH MASCARPONE
AND STILTON CREAM

———

(2) arouse-o-meter | 1 | 2 | 3 | **4** | 5 |

1 large quince ~ 200g caster sugar ~ juice of ½ lemon ~ 100g Greek yogurt ~ 100g mascarpone ~ 150g good Stilton cheese ~ 1 tsp honey

The quince was the equivalent of Viagra in Henry VIII's day, but for some reason it is not so widely used today, either as an aphrodisiac or merely as a fruit. Membrillo – a thick, slightly grainy quince paste most commonly served with Manchego cheese – is popular, and quince jelly is the preserve of WI ladies all over the country, though what they actually do with the hundreds of jars I regularly see at country fêtes is a mystery to me. I sometimes use it to sweeten game sauces instead of redcurrant jelly, but the pairing with cheese is the best.

This sort of dessert-cum-cheese course matches the dulcet tones of quince with the robust saltiness of Stilton. Try it with a glass of Sauternes or Pedro Ximénez sherry.

Milton's Method ☞ Peel the quince and slice it in half lengthways.

Measure a litre of water into a saucepan, add the sugar and lemon juice and bring to the boil.

Carefully place the quince halves in the pan, cover with a lid and simmer for 30–35 minutes or until the flesh is tender (check with a skewer or knife point).

Meanwhile, blend the Greek yogurt and mascarpone in a bowl. Crumble in the Stilton and stir well. Add the honey, mix thoroughly and place a large dollop of this cream on each plate.

When the quince halves are cooked, remove with a slotted spoon and put one on each plate, pouring over 1 tbsp of their poaching liquid to serve.

SWEET
BITS

—

Ambrosial sweetness is inherently sensual. Smearing honey, chewing chocolate and licking ice cream, for instance, are all completely erotic activities, even when you're doing them on your own. Add a potential sexual partner into the mix and the sweet ending to your meal could be the start of something equally delicious and – possibly – ambrosial, too.

It is not just the sweetness of desserts that makes them so sexy, but their textures and flavours: sticky and gooey, fruity and chocolatey. They should be platefuls of fun and frolics, indulgence and hedonism, the cause of delight and surprise. They can either be smoulderingly hot or thrillingly frosty, but they must make us either smile or swoon.

Chocolate is known as one of the great aphrodisiacs and has been used as such for centuries. But there are many other ingredients that can be used at the end of a meal to signify that the serious business of eating is done and the fun can begin. In this chapter, I will show you how spices, rose petals and honey can also be part of the sensual smorgasbord that pudding can bring to the table. Try them at this crucial stage in the evening to see if they produce the desired result.

And, as you savour the last lingering sweetness on your lips, perhaps now is the right moment to lean forward and give your partner an equally lingering kiss.

CRANACHAN

WITH FIGS, CANDIED
WALNUTS, HONEY AND
MERINGUE

———

(2) arouse-o-meter | 1 | **2** | 3 | 4 | 5 |

handful of dried figs ~ 2 tbsp honey ~ 300ml double cream ~ 50g good-quality porridge oats ~ large knob of unsalted butter ~ handful of walnuts ~ 1 tbsp granulated sugar ~ 1 heaped tbsp broken meringue pieces ~ 50ml Scotch whisky 200g raspberries

This has always seemed to me a slightly straight-laced Scottish dessert, but with the addition of a few fun bits and pieces it can — like a repressed Englishman (or Scotsman) on holiday — break free from its shackles.

Milton's Method ☞ Chop the figs, removing their stalks, and put them in a bowl. Stir in 1 tablespoon of the honey and 1 tablespoon of hot water from the kettle. Leave to soak for 30 minutes.

Whip the cream in a large bowl until it forms soft, billowing peaks.

Toast the oats in a small, non-stick pan over a medium heat for 3 or 4 minutes, taking care not to burn them. Set aside.

In the same pan, add the butter, walnuts and sugar, stir well to combine and stir for 3–4 minutes, making sure that the sugar doesn't burn. Once the sugar has caramelised, remove the nuts from the pan straight away, place them on a sheet of greaseproof paper and separate them from one another. Allow them to cool.

Fold most of the nuts and all the remaining ingredients into the cream, and that extra tablespoon of honey, and reserving a few raspberries and walnuts to serve. Serve in small bowls or glasses, sprinkling with raspberries and candied walnuts.

CHOCOLATE CHILLI FONDANT

—

(3)  (arouse-o-meter | 1 | 2 | 3 | **4** | 5)

60g good-quality dark chocolate ~ 60g unsalted butter, plus more for the moulds ~ ½ medium-hot red chilli, deseeded and finely chopped ~ 2 free-range eggs, lightly beaten ~ 75g caster sugar ~ 25g plain flour ~ icing sugar, to dust ~ a very little cayenne pepper, to dust (optional)

It may be time for dessert, but, for you lovers, I hope that the 'main course' of your dinner date is still to arrive. With this in mind, the food at the end of your meal should still be focused on exciting you rather than rocking you to sleep, titillating your palate rather than soothing it. Hence chocolate and chilli. The spice here should be subtle rather than explosive, but enough to leave a lingering heat on your tongue, a flush in your cheeks and a light sweat on your brow, as though you are already mildly aroused. You will need two dariole moulds.

Milton's Method ☞ Break the chocolate into small pieces and put into a heatproof bowl suspended over simmering water (don't allow the bowl to touch the water). Add the butter to the bowl and melt with the chocolate together. Once both are fully melted, stir once to combine, remove from the heat and add the chilli. Set aside to cool slightly.

Butter two dariole moulds and preheat the oven to 200°C/gas mark 6.

In a separate bowl, whisk the eggs and sugar together until well combined and fluffy. Gradually add the chocolate and butter mixture, stirring as you go, then fold in the flour. When everything is mixed, gently pour the batter into the prepared moulds, to reach about three-quarters of the way up.

Bake for around 7 minutes, or until there is a crust on the outside but the puddings are still molten in the middle (test with a skewer).

Loosen the fondants very carefully by squeezing a palette knife down the sides, then carefully tip on to serving plates. Dust with a little icing sugar and a very little cayenne pepper, if you like (though do go carefully and check your partner enjoys heat first, as too much could render them inedible) and serve with vanilla ice cream.

RED WINE
POACHED PEARS

WITH STEM GINGER
CRÈME FRAÎCHE

For the pears: *500ml good-quality fruity red wine, such as Italian Primitivo ~ 100ml fresh orange juice ~ 1 tbsp finely grated orange zest ~ 150g caster sugar ~ 1 vanilla pod, split ~ 2 star anise ~ 1 cinnamon stick ~ 4 cardamom pods, gently crushed ~ 2 ripe Comice pears, peeled and cut at the base so they can stand up ~ 50g unsalted butter, chopped*
For the ginger crème fraîche: *1 tbsp stem ginger syrup from the jar ~ 150g crème fraîche ~ 6 balls of stem ginger, roughly chopped*

There is something rather sensuous and beautiful about a pear poached in red wine, it looks magnificent and smells delicious. The aromatics used to achieve the flavour in this dish include vanilla, cinnamon, cardamom and star anise. This subtle, delicate spicing, along with the depth of flavour of good red wine, creates an intoxicating blend that should hopefully prove irresistible to your dinner partner. Crème fraîche cut through with pieces of stem ginger – another aphrodisiac – provides the perfect accompaniment.

Milton's Method ✒ Pour the wine and orange juice into a large lidded saucepan or casserole and add the zest, sugar and spices. Place over a medium heat, stirring until the sugar has dissolved. Add the pears so they are standing in the pan and reduce the heat to low. Place the lid on the pan and simmer for 45 minutes to 1 hour, or until the pears are soft but not falling apart (test with a knife).

Make the crème fraîche by gently combining the syrup, crème fraîche and stem ginger in a bowl. Spoon this into the centre of serving bowls. When the pears are ready, remove them from the pan and stand them in the bowls, squidging them down so the crème fraîche comes up around the base of each.

Bring the red wine sauce to the boil and reduce it until it is thick. Then remove from the heat, whisk in the butter pieces until it thickens slightly and serve warm, sprinkling a little over the pears and offering the rest in a jug on the side.

VANILLA AND SAFFRON BAGUETTE AND BUTTER PUDDING

WITH GOOSEBERRY-GINGER JAM

2 | arouse-o-meter | 1 2 3 **4** 5

30g unsalted butter, plus more for the dish ~ 2 tbsp gooseberry and ginger jam, plus more to glaze ~ ½ large baguette (about 150g) ~ 1 large free-range egg, plus 1 large free-range egg yolk ~ 25g caster sugar ~ ½ vanilla pod, split ~ 1 generous pinch of saffron threads ~ 100ml whole milk ~ 200ml double cream ~ 2 tbsp dark rum ~ 40g sultanas ~ 1 tbsp demerara sugar

Bread and butter pudding may not seem the most romantic of desserts, but by adding two exotic spices, a hit of rum and some gooseberry and ginger jam, it is elevated into a heady, fragrant dish with an indulgent texture.

Saffron threads are the female sex organs – the stigma – of crocuses. That on its own may or may not be important, but it certainly helps to set out its stall as one of the most well-known aphrodisiacs, used by Greek gods, no less, in their pursuit of female company. Zeus seduced the princess Europa by breathing saffron from his mouth. Cleopatra, it is said, bathed in large quantities of the spice before making love.

Saffron also happens to be remarkably expensive, by virtue of the fact that it is so labour-intensive to harvest, and perhaps this also adds to its reputation.

Milton's Method ☞ Preheat the oven to 180°C/gas mark 4. Butter a medium-sized rectangular ovenproof dish. Spread the jam over the base of the dish.

Slice the baguette thinly and butter both sides, then overlap the slices in the dish.

Prepare a cold custard: beat the egg, egg yolk and caster sugar in a large bowl until thickened slightly and bubbly. Scrape the seeds from the half vanilla pod into the bowl, add the saffron, then mix in the milk, cream and rum. Mix well, then slowly pour over the bread. Sprinkle the sultanas over the pudding and leave for 30 minutes so the custard soaks into the bread.

Place the dish in a larger baking tray and pour boiling water around it. Sprinkle with the demerara sugar and, taking great care that the hot water doesn't spill, bake in the oven for around 35 minutes until golden on top.

Remove from the oven. Melt a little more jam in a small saucepan with a splash of hot water to loosen, then brush this glaze over the pudding. Leave to stand for 10 minutes before serving.

RASPBERRY AND ROSE PUDDING

—

2 | arouse-o-meter | 1 | **2** | 3 | 4 | 5 |

For the pudding: *1 tbsp cornflour ~ pinch of fine salt ~ 1 free-range egg yolk ~ 250g raspberries ~ 50g caster sugar ~ juice of ½ lemon ~ 150ml double cream*
~ 1 tsp edible rose water **To serve:** *1 tbsp white chocolate curls ~ 1 tbsp edible dried rose petals ~ 1 tbsp lightly crushed freeze-dried raspberries ~ 4 chocolate wafer sticks*

I remember as a child sniffing deep red roses and thinking that they also smelt of raspberries. I discovered, while researching this book, that rose is a noted aphrodisiac… and its associations with romance, of course, are as enduring as they are clichéd. So the first thing that sprung to mind when I thought of using flowers in this book was to make a dessert out of raspberries and roses. And it works. The raspberries really shine through at first taste and the rose lingers a little (but not cloyingly) at the end.

Milton's Method ☞ Mix the cornflour and salt in a large bowl, then slowly pour in 125ml of water, whisking all the time until smooth. Add the egg yolk and whisk until fully incorporated.

Put the raspberries, sugar and lemon juice in a blender and liquidise until smooth. Strain the mixture through a sieve to get rid of the seeds and pour into a heavy-based saucepan. Heat the mixture, stirring all the time, until it comes to the boil. Reduce the heat to its lowest, then take a couple of tbsp of the warm raspberry purée and whisk it into the bowl with the cornflour mixture. When it is well blended, pour back into the saucepan with the rest of the raspberry purée, whisking all the time, until the mixture has thickened and changed in colour from dark red to pink. Keeping the pan over a low heat, return to the boil, simmer for a couple of minutes to cook out the cornflour, whisking as you go, then set aside.

In a separate bowl, whisk the double cream until it forms billowing soft peaks but is not stiff, then whisk in the rose water. Once the raspberry mixture has cooled a little, fold in the cream until it is completely blended. Spoon the pudding immediately into serving dishes – I suggest either martini glasses, ramekins or small bowls – cover with cling film and place in the fridge. Leave for at least 2 hours to chill.

When you are ready to serve, sprinkle with white chocolate curls, rose petals and crushed freeze dried raspberries, placing a couple of chocolate wafer sticks on the side.

Acknowledgements

This book would not have been written without a number of important people. Rosemary Davidson at Square Peg inspired the idea and Susannah Otter has been an organised and enthusiastic editor who has kept everything on track against some challenging deadlines. Lucy Bannell is a fantastic copy editor who has pointed out many important issues with a number of recipes and Marion Moisy tightened the text up still further at the proofreading stage. As ever, my brilliant agent Andrew Gordon has helped work out the details between everyone, and his assistant David Evans has been a great help in sorting out contracts and the like.

The dynamic duo of Matt Baxter and Graeme Rodrigo have played an instrumental role, not just in their respective fields of illustration and design, but in coming up with ideas for the whole concept. Katie Morgan's beautiful watercolour illustrations are also a vital part of the book.

I would also like to thank Tom Charman for the fantastic venison and Price's Butchers for their excellent meat. Thanks to Bridget, Gilbert and Rafe for trying out many of the recipes, to Sue Telfer for testing the banana cake and Hilary Chandler for testing the fried oyster recipe.

It is patently absurd (they can't even read!) but I would also like to thank my three hens Delhi, Naggar and Leh, who have provided me with a plentiful supply of eggs during the writing of a book that has used vast quantities of them.

Despite help from all these people (and chickens), if there are any errors or omissions, they are mine alone.